Patsy Clark

Problem-Based Learning
A Collection of Articles

Edited by
Robin Fogarty

SkyLight
Professional
Development

Arlington Heights, Illinois

Problem-Based Learning: A Collection of Articles

Published by SkyLight Professional Development
2626 S. Clearbrook Dr., Arlington Heights, IL 60005-5310
800-348-4474 or 847-290-6600
Fax 847-290-6609
info@skylightedu.com
http://www.skylightedu.com

Creative Director: Robin Fogarty
Managing Editor: Ela Aktay
Editor: Amy Kinsman
Acquisitions Editor: Jean Ward
Type Compositor: Donna Ramirez
Cover Designer: David Stockman
Book Designer: Donna Ramirez
Production Supervisor: Bob Crump

Printed in the United States of America.
ISBN 1-57517-047-7

LCCCN: 97-62451

2115-V
Item number 1529

Z Y X W V U T S R Q P O N M L K J I H G F E D
06 05 04 03 02 01   15 14 13 12 11 10 9 8 7 6 5 4

ontents

Introduction

Problem-Based Learning
A Collection of Articles

We are confronted by a condition, not a theory.

—Grover Cleveland

Problem-based learning (PBL) is the search for solutions to life's messy problems. It is learning by encountering the perplexing, the bewildering, the dilemmas of real-world problems. PBL is about becoming immersed, as stakeholders, in problematic situations and addressing the concerns with empathy. It is about understanding the circumstances and the subsequent consequences of actions taken. PBL is learning in its most authentic state. It is the real world.

More specifically, PBL is an elegant design for learning that begins with an ill-structured or open-ended problem scenario. What do middle schoolers need to know to survive and flourish in their careers of choice? How might the power of the waterways be harnessed without polluting the cities and countryside? PBL is inquiry learning. The investigations that develop, strand by strand, thread by thread, continue until appropriate and acceptable solutions emerge. Throughout the PBL unit, the learner directs the design of the web of inquiry and, ultimately, is responsible for its final architecture.

To explore the true nature of problem-based learning as a curricular framework and an instructional model for kindergarten through college classrooms, this collection of articles has been assembled. It provides a broad perspective to the concept of PBL and is intended as an introductory volume on the issues, for the professional library of today's informed educator.

Through a spectrum of articles that range from a historical perspective of PBL to the theoretical underpinnings that validate the model for schooling, to a more practical vision of uses in the regular classroom and in special applications, this collection presents PBL as a viable alternative to traditional curriculum. It is a pocket guide for the busy professional who wants to know more about PBL or for those who may want to create study groups to explore the nature and nuances of the model.

Section 1

Beginnings . . .
Problem-Based Learning

Probe the earth, and see where your main roots run.
—Henry David Thoreau

While the opening section is comprised of a single article, its scope broadly encompasses the historical roots of problem-based learning (PBL) as a medical model. Bridges and Hallinger present a comprehensive review of the literature on PBL in medical education and make a case for using PBL in schools of education for preparing administrators.

In their paper, *Problem-Based Learning in Medical and Managerial Education,* they delineate five defining characters of PBL: it is the starting point for learning, the problem is one that students are apt to encounter in their future work, subject matter is organized around problems rather than disciplines, students assume a major role in their learning, and most learning occurs within the context of small groups.

In addition, eight design issues are addressed: PBL's incorporation into the curriculum, selection and definition of problems, identification of goals, components of small group learning, program planning, evaluation, student orientation, and faculty preparation. Within the context of these eight issues, a research agenda is proposed and educators are encouraged to tackle the challenges of moving from a traditional approach to a PBL approach.

While its original intent was not solely to provide a historical perspective in the sense that it is used in this collection, the discussion serves this serendipitous purpose nicely. To begin the readings with this well-supported research seems to, in turn, serve the reader well.

Problem-Based Learning in Medical and Managerial Education

by Edwin M. Bridges and Phillip Hallinger[1]

The preparation of school administrators currently occupies centerstage on the intellectual agenda of professors and departments of educational administration (Griffiths, Stout and Forsyth, 1988). One manifestation of this new found interest in preparing administrators is a proposal to increase the relevance of preparation by orienting it more explicitly to problems of practice. This proposal, like many others, lacks specificity and skirts the issue of whether it is supported by theory, research, or both.

The present chapter seeks to fill this gap by drawing on the problem-based learning (PBL) literature in the field of medical education. As we shall see, medical educators throughout the world use problem-based learning to train physicians. Moreover, medical educators have studied this instructional approach extensively. Their experience offers us a unique opportunity to build on and go beyond what they have learned as we apply this promising approach to preparing educational administrators.[2]

PROBLEM-BASED LEARNING IN MEDICAL EDUCATION

Problem-based learning is used in more than 80 percent of the medical schools in the United States (Jonas, Etzel and Barzansky, 1989) and has five defining characteristics:

1. The starting point for learning is a problem.
2. The problem is one that students are to apt face as future physicians.

3.   Subject matter is organized around problems rather than the disciplines.

4.   Students assume a major responsibility for their own instruction and learning.

5.   Most learning occurs within the context of small groups rather than lectures.

Apart from these five common features, problem-based learning curricula in medical schools vary along the following two dimensions: (1) the program's major goals (e.g., knowledge acquisition and use, problem-solving skills, and self-directed learning skills) and (2) the extent to which the instructors or the students choose the learning objectives, resources, and models of student evaluation.

Rationale

Medical educators justify using problem-based learning on grounds which, in our judgment, apply with equal force to the preparation of school administrators. First, medical educators contend and buttress their contention with empirical evidence that medical students retain little of what they learn in the basic disciplines (Bok 1989). Second, medical educators cite research which shows that students in medicine and a host of other fields often do not appropriately use the knowledge which they have learned (Schmidt 1983). (We suspect that researchers in the field of educational administration would find similar results in both instances.) Third, since students forget much of what is learned or use their knowledge inappropriately, instructors should create conditions that optimize retrieval and appropriate use of the knowledge in future professional practice.

> Medical educators justify using problem-based learning . . .

Fourth, PBL creates the three conditions which information theory links to subsequent retrieval and appropriate use of new information (Schmidt, 1983):

a.   *Prior knowledge is activated,* i.e., students apply knowledge they already possess in order to understand the new information. This prior knowledge and the kind of structure in which it is stored determine what is understood from the new experience and what is learned from it. Problems are selected and sequenced to ensure that this activation of prior knowledge occurs.

b. *The context in which information is learned resembles the context in which it will later be applied* (referred to as encoding specificity). Research shows that knowledge is much more likely to be remembered or recalled in the context in which it was originally learned (Godden and Baddeley, 1975). Encoding specificity in problem-based learning is achieved by having students acquire knowledge in a functional context, i.e., in a context containing problems that closely resemble the problems which they will encounter later in their professional career.

c. *Information is better understood, processed and recalled if students have an opportunity to elaborate on that information.* Elaborations provide redundancy in the memory structure which in turn reduces forgetting and abets retrieval. Elaboration occurs in problem-based learning in various ways, namely, discussing the subject matter with other students, teaching peers what they first learned themselves, exchanging views about how the information applies to the problem they are seeking to solve, and preparing essays about what they have learned while seeking to solve the problem.

Fifth, PBL explicitly forces students to adopt a problem-solving orientation when learning new information.

> The advantage of such an approach is that students become much more aware of how the knowledge they are acquiring can be put to use. Adopting a problem-solving mentality, even when it is marginally appropriate, reinforces the notion that the knowledge is useful for achieving particular goals. Students are not being asked to store information away; they see how it works in certain situations which increases the accessibility. (Prawat, 1989, p. 18)

Finally, the disciples of PBL stress the motivational value of the approach. They maintain that students enjoy the opportunity to play the role of doctor during their preclinical training and find the activity of working on simulated patient problems intrinsically rewarding.

Empirical evidence

Although medical educators present a rather persuasive rationale for using PBL to train a physician, do they provide any evidence that the approach is a sound one? *Yes, compared with traditional programs in medical education, PBL programs generally yield equal or superior results.* The results are summarized below.

Students in PBL programs express substantially more positive attitudes toward their training than do students in more traditional programs. The former praise their training, especially those aspects which are unique to problem-based learning, while the latter often describe their training as boring, irrelevant, and anxiety-provoking (deVries, Schmidt, and deGraaff, 1989; and Schmidt, Dauphinee, Patel, 1987).

Besides expressing more favorable attitudes toward their education, students in PBL programs also adopt more desirable approaches to studying than their traditional program counterparts. PBL students are more likely to adopt a *meaning orientation* to studying, i.e., to be intrinsically motivated by the subject matter and to strive to understand the material. Students in traditional programs, on the other hand, are more likely to adopt a *reproducing orientation* to studying, i.e., use rote learning and seek to reproduce the factual information in the syllabus (Coles, 1985; deVolder and deGrave, 1989; Schmidt, Dauphinee, and Patel, 1987).

> Besides expressing more favorable attitudes toward their education, students in PBL programs also adopt more desirable approaches to studying . . .

These differences in attitudes and approaches to studying also translate into differences in rates and time of completion. In countries with relatively high dropout rates among medical students, students in PBL programs are much more likely to graduate and to complete their programs of study in less time than students in traditional programs (deVries, Schmidt, and deGraaff, 1989).

Students in PBL programs also tend to perform better than students in conventional programs on measures of problem solving proficiency and clinical competence (deVries, Schmidt, and deGraaff, 1989; Jones et al., 1986; Kaufman, et al., 1989; and Schmidt, Dauphinee, and Patel, 1987). However, we should note that the performance differences are small and that the outcome measures vary in quality.

When medical knowledge is considered, the pattern of differences reverses itself. Students in conventional programs score slightly higher on standardized tests of medical knowledge than students in PBL programs (Schmidt, et al., 1989; deVries, Schmidt, and deGraaff, 1989; and Kaufman, et al., 1989). The differences are small enough that they are of little practical importance.

Limitations of the research on PBL

The research that has been conducted on the effectiveness of problem-based learning versus the traditional approach is flawed in several respects. Let us examine the deficiencies of this research in terms of the specification of the independent variable and the measurement of dependent variables.

Independent variable

Although researchers claim that they are contrasting problem-based learning with traditional training programs, their claims are suspect. There are virtually no attempts to define what is meant by "traditional." Moreover, when problem-based learning is compared with the traditional approach, PBL often is not the main instructional approach. In those cases where PBL appears to be the main approach and is explicitly defined, it is clear that the PBL programs belong to the same genus but different species.

Measures of the dependent variables

The measures of the dependent variables, like the specification of the independent variable, are also suspect. Researchers rarely cite any evidence that attests to the reliability of the measures. In those rare instances where the research supplies data about reliability (Imbos, et al., 1984; deVolder and deGrave, 1989), the coefficients are moderate at best (.26 to less than .80).

When measuring differences in medical knowledge (e.g., deVries, Schmidt, and deGraaff, 1989; Jones, et al., 1984; and Kaufman, et al., 1989), researchers appear to be testing recall via cued questions (i.e., alternative answers furnished), rather than recall and spontaneous use of knowledge in clinical contexts. Given the rationale for problem-based learning in medial education, its seems more appropriate to measure how well students retrieve and correctly use knowledge in clinical contexts without external prompts (Claessen and Boshuizen, 1985).

Unlike medical knowledge, problem-solving proficiency is measured in the context of patient problems. Researchers supply medical students with bits of information about patients and then ask the students to reproduce as much of this information as possible. Their proficiency in problem-solving is assessed in terms of how many items of information they correctly recall and the degree to which the information is structured or randomly reproduced. This mode of assessment represents a limited measure of problem-solving proficiency—efficiency in encoding and chunking information that is used in solving problems.

DESIGNING PROBLEM-BASED LEARNING PROGRAMS FOR EDUCATIONAL ADMINISTRATORS

As we have indicated, there is ample, though not conclusive, evidence that PBL equals or is superior to traditional instructional approaches in producing desirable outcomes for medical education. In light of these promising results, we think it is important to experiment with different forms of problem-based learning in preparing administrators. To facilitate this experimentation, we have identified eight major design issues that represent possibilities for developing and studying different PBL program designs. In the discussion that follows we discuss these various issues and what we have learned about them through our reading and our own efforts at Stanford and Vanderbilt Universities to prepare aspiring and practicing administrators using PBL.

> ... there is ample, though not conclusive, evidence that PBL equals or is superior to traditional instructional approaches ...

Issue 1: How should PBL be incorporated into the curriculum?

There are at least four different ways PBL can be incorporated into the curriculum for preparing educational administrators (1) PBL can be used as the main instructional approach for the entire curriculum; (2) the curriculum can consist of two tracks with one of these tracks using PBL as the main approach; (3) one or more courses in the curriculum can be organized around problem-based learning; and (4) a portion of one or more courses can use PBL.

The first alternative appears to be the least desirable choice for several reasons. Although students apparently enjoy the approach, it is clear that some students prefer a more traditional learning format (Jones, et al., 1984). Other students like the variety reflected in programs employing both traditional and PBL approaches. Instructors, like students, differ in their preferences for traditional and problem-based learning. These differences may lead to needless, destructive conflict within departments of educational administration. Finally, problem-based learning, though a promising alternative, remains an unproven method in preparing educational administrators. Since its

effectiveness remains in doubt, trials on a more limited basis seem
warranted.

Issue 2: What problems should be used, and how should they be presented?

Since problems are one of the defining characteristics of the genus,
PBL, program designers need to devote considerable time and
thought to this second issue. When choosing focal problems for the
PBL curriculum, one or more of the following criteria may be used:
(1) *prevalence* (i.e., the problem is a common one); (2) *integrative
value* (i.e., the problem is suitable for studying concepts from a range
of disciplines); (3) *prototypic value* (i.e., the problem, though rare, is
an excellent model for study); (4) *high potential impact* (i.e., the
problem threatens large numbers of people for an extended period
of time); and (5) *lack of structure* (i.e., the problem is a "swamp"
with many issues and sub-issues).

When presenting the focal problems to students, these problems
can be presented as a written case, a live role play, an interactive
computer simulation, interactive videodisc, or a taped episode. Sole
reliance on written cases or verbal vignettes, as Bransford, et al.
(1989) have noted, may have dysfunctional consequences for the
learner. In order to become an expert, a great deal of perceptual
learning must occur and this cannot happen unless the student
learns to recognize the salient visual, auditory, and non-verbal cues.
When designing a PBL curriculum, program designers should strive
for a variety of modalities in presenting problems to educational administrators. If students encounter only verbal descriptions of problems, they may be unprepared to deal with real problems.

Issue 3: What should be the goals of problem-based learning for educational administrators?

There are at least four major goals which may lie at the heart of
problem-based learning: (1) acquisition of retrievable and usable
knowledge; (2) problem-solving skills; (3) administrative skills; and
(4) self-directed learning skills. Since most professors of educational
administration are quite familiar with the rationale for the three
goals, we will limit our discussion to the goal of self-directed learning
skills. This goal rarely surfaces in discussions of curriculum in our
field; moreover, it represents the most important and problematic
choice for PBL designers.

The rationale underlying the need for self-directed learning skills is straightforward. The knowledge base that undergirds professional practice is vast and continually undergoing change. If professionals are to keep abreast of this knowledge base, they need to acquire skills in learning how to learn. These self-directed learning skills include: proficiency in identifying one's own learning needs and objectives; skill in locating and evaluating resources (reference material and expert advice); competence in applying the knowledge to professional problems; and skill in self-evaluation.

The decision to make self-directed learning skills a major goal is a crucial design decision. If designers decide to emphasize these skills, many of the subsequent design decisions will be made by the student, rather than by the instructional staff. These design decisions include the specific learning objectives, the relevant resources, and the modes of evaluation. When designers turn these decisions over to students, two risks arise. First, there is limited evidence that students select learning objectives which do not always correspond to the ones envisioned by the instructional staff (who, in turn, may be responding to the program requirements of state accreditation agencies). There is some overlap, but it is less than perfect. Second, when given the opportunity to define their own learning needs and resources, students, in our experience, may transform PBL into a library research project. If this happens, students devote more time and effort to summarizing what they have learned, rather than to applying the knowledge to the focal problem.

> The decision to make self-directed learning skills a major goal is a crucial design decision.

Issue 4: How should the small learning groups be constituted?

One of the defining characteristics of PBL is that the primary learning format is a small group. These small groups may be consisted as a tutorial (Barrows, 1984), a cooperative learning group (Slavin, 1989), or a project team. Our experience, thus far, leads us to favor constituting the small group as a project team, but the other two ways remain viable choices.

Each project team consists of five to seven students; the instructor is not a member of the team but serves as a resource to it. Since administrators frequently administer projects, the small group affords students with an opportunity to develop an array of skills associated with project management. Most notably, students learn skills in planning how to accomplish the project's goals in a fixed period of time with existing resources. In addition, students learn what is involved in shouldering responsibility for carrying out a plan with the members of a project team. By varying the goals, the composition of the team, the leader, and the duration of the project, PBL designers are able to expose students to the situational nature of leadership and the risk and the uncertainty that are characteristic of managerial work. Project meetings also provide opportunities for students to acquire competence in running meetings, a major medium of managerial work.

> ... PBL designers are able to expose students to the situational nature of leadership and the risk and the uncertainty that are characteristic of managerial work.

Issue 5: How much should each focal problem (or problem-based learning project) be pre-structured?

When designing a PBL program for educational administrators, designers may elect to provide varying amounts of prestructuring for each focal problem or project. At one extreme, the designer may supply only the problem and permit students to define the rest of the structure (i.e., the learning objectives, the resources, and the model of evaluation). At the other extreme, the designer may provide the problem and specify the learning objectives, resources, guiding questions (either to highlight certain concepts or to help the student analyze the problem), and mode of evaluation. Between these two extremes, the designer can vary the degree of pre-structuring by allowing students to decide one or more of the following: learning objectives, learning resources, and mode of evaluation.

How much pre-structuring occurs depends upon two factors. The first factor involves the major goals of the program. If the designer wishes to emphasize self-directed learning skills, each project is likely to reflect a minimal amount of pre-structuring. If, however, the designer attaches little or no importance to self-directed learning skills, each project is apt to be highly pre-structured. A second factor relates to the availability of resources; the less students have easy access to a library and relevant experts, the greater the need for pre-structuring the learning objectives and resources.

Even if the designer elects to emphasize self-directed learning skills, it is important to pre-structure the focal problems or projects during the early stages. Students find it difficult to make the transition to a problem-based learning program, and the transition is sometimes slow. Accordingly, projects need to be pre-structured at the outset with the amount of pre-structuring being gradually reduced as students become more comfortable and more familiar with problem-based learning.

Issue 6: What form should evaluation take in the context of problem-based learning?

When grappling with this issue, designers need to distinguish between program and student evaluation and between formative and summative evaluation. In the early stages of implementing PBL, we have found it valuable to emphasize formative evaluation. Despite our efforts to create units that are flawless from the outset, we inevitably learn from the initial field tests of these projects. Student feedback, supplemented by our own observations, leads to revision. In some cases these revisions are substantial. The second trial of the unit or project generally results in little or no revision. Once the problem-based learning projects have been field-tested and debugged, it is appropriate and desirable to conduct summative evaluations.

When conducting formative or summative evaluations of student performance, designers may use one or more methods to assess the quality of a student's performance. The most commonly used methods in medical education are self-evaluation, peer evaluation, and instructor evaluation. We have followed the practices used in medical education and have used all three methods to evaluate student performance.

Issue 7: How should students be prepared to function effectively in a problem-based learning instructional environment?

As we have noted, students encounter difficulty in making the transition from a traditional to a problem-based learning environment. Medical educators have alluded to these difficulties, and we have observed them as we have worked with aspiring and practicing administrators. If designers properly attend to transitional issues, they can reduce the stress experienced by students and can accelerate their successful adjustment to this instructional approach.

To ease the students' transition to a problem-based learning environment, designers have several options. Besides extensively pre-structuring the first few problem-based units, designers can provide students with an orientation to problem-based learning and with some of the foundational skills the process requires. Based on our experience, we have found it helpful to orient students by describing PBL in relation to the following questions: What is problem-based learning? What is the underlying rationale for PBL? How will PBL be incorporated into their training? What are the major goals? How will the learning groups be constituted? How will students be evaluated? In other words, students need to know how the instructional staff has decided to resolve the various design issues.

> ... it is important to provide formal training in designing and implementing PBL ...

The students' transitions to PBL can also be facilitated by providing them with training in the kinds of skills which they will need to succeed in a problem-based curriculum. For the most part, these skills are the same ones which they will need when they become administrators—skills in project and meeting management, problem-solving, conflict resolution, and oral and written communication. Acquisition of these skills is enhanced through their repeated use in the problem-based learning units. Depending upon the major goals of the curriculum, students may also need training in locating and evaluating relevant published materials.

Issue 8: How should faculty be prepared to function effectively in a problem-based learning environment?

Even if faculty members favor using a problem-based learning approach, they are likely to encounter difficulty in making the transition. The vast majority of faculty members have been prepared in disciplinary-based programs that rely heavily on two methods—the lecture and instructor-led discussions. Having limited or no exposure to the problem-based approach, faculty members understandably will lack some of the basic knowledge and skills needed to design a PBL program and to implement it successfully. Under these conditions, it is important to provide formal training in designing and implementing PBL and to create settings in which instructors can share their difficulties and discuss ways of dealing with them.

PBL: A FUTURE RESEARCH AGENDA

Since problem-based learning is a promising, but unproven, approach for preparing educational administrators, it represents a potentially fruitful area for investigation. To stimulate interest in studying this instructional approach, we will suggest some directions that research on problem-based learning might take.

Proposed Focus

In our judgment, the educational administration research community should re-frame the basic question asked by researchers in medical education. As we indicated earlier, medical educators generally seek to answer some form of the following question: Do problem-based learning programs produce significantly better outcomes for medical students than traditional programs? A more appropriate and potentially more illuminating question is as follows: How effective are the various species of PBL in achieving the different goals of managerial education?

This particular question is more desirable for several reasons. First, this formulation recognizes that there is no agreement among PBL supporters about what problem-based learning means. Second, this formulation acknowledges that we do not currently understand which elements of PBL or combination of elements are effective in achieving different types of educational goals. This important issue continues to baffle medical educators because of the way in which they have posed their basic research question. Finally, this way of framing the question is less divisive because it does not pit advocates of PBL against the proponents of more established, traditional approaches. As a result, there is likely to be a greater willingness within departments of educational administration to experiment with problem-based learning.

Independent Variables

Program evaluators do not commonly "describe fully, let alone measure, how the programs in 'experimental' and 'control' situations actually differ from one another—or even to certify that they do." (Charters and Jones, 1975, p. 342) We noted this phenomenon in the research on PBL in medical education and pointed out the consequences, namely, the uninterpretability of the results.

In light of what Charters and Jones have noted and what we have observed during our review of research on PBL, we fear that history may repeat itself. To prevent this from happening, PBL researchers in the field of educational administration should specify which species of PBL they are studying. As we have indicated earlier in this paper, these species can be described in terms of how the faculty chose to resolve each of the eight design issues which we highlighted. In addition, researchers should certify that the PBL programs actually operated as they were described. Descriptive studies of how one or more elements (e.g., the small learning groups and the role of the instructor) in the PBL design was implemented would be especially informative.

> Students who learned the information under a problem-processing format were much more likely to use this information spontaneously in developing action plans . . .

Dependent Variables

The choice of dependent variable depends primarily on the major goals of the program. PBL programs may, as we have noted, emphasize one or more of the following goals: retrievable/usable knowledge, problem-solving skills, administrative skills, and self-directed learning skills. We will limit our discussion to the two goals which have received the greatest attention by medical researchers, namely, knowledge and problem-solving skills.

In studying the degree to which the knowledge goal has been accomplished, researchers could profitably follow the lead of Bransford, et al. (1989). These cognitive psychologists have studied the spontaneous use of knowledge by college students who acquired information under problem-processing and fact-processing instructional formats. Students who learned the information under a problem-processing format were much more likely to use this information spontaneously in developing action plans than students taught the same information in a fact-processing format. Bransford's work provides a potentially fruitful approach to studying knowledge use and suggest that one or more versions of problem-based learning is likely to be effective in promoting the retrieval and use of knowledge. Alternatively, researchers might examine knowledge retrieval and use in clinical contexts (e.g., internship or on-the-job).

Studying the effects of PBL on administrator problem-solving skills represents a more formidable challenge. "There are no simple tricks to assessing problem-solving skills." (McGuire, 1980, p. 122)

The absence of a single yardstick for assessing problem-solving proficiency leads us to propose several approaches to this important, but admittedly complex, task. What the intellectual yield will be from these various approaches remains a mystery.

Medical educators have tended to assess the effectiveness of problem-solving skills by examining the efficiency of medical students in encoding and chunking information gleaned from simulated patient problems. If this approach were used in the field of educational administration, researchers would ask students to read a case and then to write down all the information they can remember. The efficiency of students in processing the information contained in the case could be gauged by scoring (a) the number of correctly reproduced items of information in the student's recall protocol and (b) the degree to which similar items are grouped together. This approach allows insight into the content and structure of the student's relevant knowledge base, a crucial factor in the ability to solve problems (Claessen and Boshuizen, 1985).

A second approach to studying problem-solving skills is suggested by the work of cognitive psychologists. There is some evidence that knowledge of general mental strategies remains inert, i.e., used only in a restricted set of contexts even though they are applicable in a wide variety of domains (Bransford, et al., 1986). In view of this possibility, researchers may find it fruitful to examine the extent to which graduates of PBL programs spontaneously use the general problem-solving strategies which they acquired during their training.

Another approach might focus on the proficiency of those individuals who spontaneously use their newly acquired problem-solving strategies. Studies of clinical reasoning reveal "that physicians often fail to collect the data they need, to pay attention to the data they do collect, . . . and to incorporate a systematic consideration of alternative risks and values in the actions they take." (McGuire, 1985, p. 594)

Administrators are also likely to reveal disquieting defects in their problem-solving processes. Based on our experience, we anticipate that students may bog down as they try to define messy, ill-structure problems and may overlook the need to anticipate the problems and obstacles which may arise when they implement a chosen course of action.

The adequacy of an administrator's problem-solving skills can also be assessed by examining the outcomes. A key assumption underlies the emphasis on general problem-solving strategies, namely, the use of these strategies leads to higher quality decisions and outcomes. The assumption needs to be tested. One way of testing it is by looking at the degree of post-decisional regret that accompanies major decisions (Janis and Mann, 1977). Presumably, a person who lacks proficiency in using problem-solving strategies when making consequential decisions will experience more post-decisional regret than one who possesses this proficiency.

> ... a person who lacks proficiency in using problem-solving strategies when making consequential decisions will experience more post-decisional regret ...

SUMMARY AND CONCLUSION

According to the critics, current programs for preparing educational administrators are inadequate and should be overhauled. These same critics propose a number of solutions to improve these preparatory programs. One of these proposals calls for increasing the relevance of administrator preparation by making it more problem-based. This proposal, sensible on its face, offers the profession a unique opportunity to build on the work of educators in other fields who are using problem-based learning (PBL) to train practitioners.

To capitalize on this opportunity, we have reviewed the literature on PBL in medical education. Our review highlights the rationale for his approach and reveals that PBL, compared with traditional programs in medical education, yields superior or equivalent results on a variety of outcome measures. Based on this review and our own personal experiences with PBL, we have identified eight major design issues which confront those who desire to use problem-based learning in preparing educational administrators. We have also proposed a research agenda aimed at increasing the field's understanding of the effectiveness of PBL in educating school administrators.

Hopefully, our discussion will stimulate others to tackle the intellectual challenges inherent in moving from a traditional to a problem-based learning approach. Those who do rise to confront these challenges are likely to experience the same kind of excitement and renewed fervor for teaching that we and others have experienced.

NOTES

1. Edwin Bridges is Professor of Education in the School of Education, Stanford University. Phillip Hallinger is Associate Professor of Education and Director of the Center for Advanced Study of Educational Leadership in Peabody College. Work on this project was supported by grants from the Walter S. Johnson Foundation and the Danforth Foundation. This paper appears in the volume, *Cognitive Perspectives on School Leadership:* New York: Teachers College Press, 1993.

2. See E. Bridges with assistance of P. Hallinger, *Problem-Based Learning for Administrators* (Eugene, Oregon: ERIC Clearinghouse for Educational Management, 1992) for numerous examples of how PBL may be incorporated into a curriculum for preparing administrators.

REFERENCES

Barrows, H., "A Specific Problem-based, Self-Directed Learning Method Designed to Teach Medical Problem-solving Skills, and Enhance Knowledge Retention" in H. Schmidt and M. deVolder (eds.), *Tutorials,* 16–32.

Bok, D. "Needed: A New Way to Train Doctors" in Schmidt, et al. (eds.) *New Directions for Medical Education,* pp. 17–38, 1989.

Bransford, J., Franks, J., Vye, N. and Sherwood, R., "New Approaches to Instruction: Because Wisdom Can't Be Told" in S. Vosniadou and M. Ortony (Eds.), *Similarity and analogical reasonings.* New York: Cambridge University Press, 1989, pp. 470–497.

Bransford, J., et al. "Teaching Thinking and Problem Solving," *American Psychologist,* 41, 10 (October 1986), 1078–1089.

Charters, W. and Jones, J. "On the Neglect of the Independent Variable in Program Evaluation" in J. Baldridge and T. Deal (eds.), *Managing Change in Educational Organizations,* Berkeley, CA: McCutchan, 1975.

Claessen, H. and Boshuizen, H., "Recall of Medical Information by Students and Doctors," *Medical Education,* 1985, 19, 61–67.

Coles, C., "Differences between Conventional and Problem-based Curricula in Their Students' Approaches to Studying," *Medical Education,* 1985, 19, 308–309.

deVolder, M. and deGrave, W., "Approaches to Learning in a Problem-based Medical Programme: A Developmental Study," *Medical Education,* 1989, 23, 262–264.

deVries, M., Schmidt, H. and deGraaff, E., "Dutch Comparisons: Cognitive and Motivational Effects of Problem-based Learning on Medical Students" in H. Schmidt, et al. *New Directions for Medical Education,* 1989, 231–238.

Godden, D. and Baddeley, A. "Context-dependent memory in two natural environments: on land and underwater," *British Journal of Psychology,* 66, 1975, 325–32.

Griffiths, D., Stout, R., and Forsyth, P. *Leaders for America's Schools.* Berkeley, CA: McCutchan Publishing Corporation, 1988.

Imbos, T., et al., "The Growth in Knowledge of Anatomy in a Problem-based Curriculum" in H. Schmidt and M. deVolder (eds.), *Tutorials,* 106–115.

Janis, I. and Mann, L. *Decision Making.* New York: The Free Press, 1977.

Jonas, H., Etzel, S. and Barzansky, B., "Undergraduate Medical Education," *JAMA,* 262, 8 (August 25, 1989), 1011–1019.

Jones, J., et al., "A Problem-based Curriculum—Ten Years of Experience" in H. Schmidt and M. deVolder (eds.), *Tutorials,* 181–198.

Kaufman, A. *Implementing Problem-Based Medical Education.* New York: Springer Publishing Company, 1985.

Kaufman, A., et al., "The New Mexico Experiment: Educational Innovation and Institutional Change," *Academic Medicine,* June 1989 Supplement, 285–294.

McGuire, C. "Medical Problem-Solving: A Critique of the Literature," *Journal of Medical Education,* 60, 8 (August, 1985), 587–595.

McGuire, C. "Assessment of Problem-Solving Skills, 2," *Medical Teacher,* 2, 3 (1980), 118–122.

Norman, G. "Problem-solving skills, solving problems and problem-based learning," *Medical Education,* 1988, 22, 279–286.

Prawat, R. "Promoting access to knowledge, strategies, and disposition in students: A research synthesis," *Review of Educational Research,* 59 (1), pp. 1–41.

Schmidt, H. "Problem-based Learning: Rationale and Description," *Medical Education,* 1983, 17, 11–16.

Schmidt, H., and deVolder, M. *Tutorials in Problem-Based Learning.* Maastricht, Netherlands: Van Gorcum, 1984.

Schmidt, H., et al. *New Directions for Medical Education.* New York: Springer-Verlag, 1989.

Schmidt, H., Dauphinee, W. and Patel, V., "Comparing the Effects of Problem-based and Conventional Curricula in an International Sample," *Journal of Medical Education,* 62 (April 1987), 305–315.

Slavin, R. "Cooperative Learning and Student Achievement" in *School and Classroom Organization,* edited by R. Slavin, N.J.: Prentice-Hall, 1989, 129–156.

Walton, H. and Matthews, M., "Essentials of problem-based learning," *Medical Education,* 23, 1989, 542–558.

Section 2

Understandings . . .
Problem-Based Learning

> *Intelligence is knowing what to do when you don't know what to do.*
>
> —Arthur L. Costa

E ntitled, *Understandings . . . Problem-Based Learning,* this next section of essays focuses on the theoretical constructs of authentic learning and the reasons behind the movement toward more student-centered learning, such as problem-based learning (PBL). Based on the premise of learning for deep understanding, the collected pieces offer insight into the constructivist theory of learning and the value of authentic, hands-on approaches in today's world of virtual reality. In essence, the discussions that comprise this section provide critical understandings for the reader about the rationale and pedagogical underpinnings of PBL.

"On Teaching for Understanding: A Conversation With Howard Gardner," is the lead piece in this discussion. Authored by Ron Brandt in an interview format, Gardner makes a case for preserving the imagination and the questioning of the five-year-old mind and at the same time, extending this natural curiosity into well-founded theories and accurate conceptions. He laments the current state of things in learning scenarios in which he feels, "Students do not *understand,* in the most basic sense of that term" (p. 4) but, rather, fall into the "correct answer compromise," in which students appear to understand because of the way they answer on a test. In the ensuing discussion, Gardner confirms that "the five-year-old mind has theories; theories of mind, theories of matter, theories of life, theories of self" (p. 5), some of which are accurate and some of which are total misconceptions. He concludes with some idea about how schools might sustain the valued learner qualities.

In a second essay on engaging learners to use their minds well, Newmann and Wehlage discuss "Five Standards of Authentic Instruction." While this article is often quoted and well on its way to becoming a classic piece in any and all constructivist's dialogues, it is included here as a guide for learning that is significant and meaningful—a distinctive quality of PBL. Included in the standards for authentic learning are higher-order thinking, depth of know-ledge, connectedness to the world beyond the classroom, substantive conversation, and social support for student achievement. Again, the relatedness of these qualities to PBL dictate inclusion of this conver-sation in the collection.

Yet, another article that provides insight and understandings about PBL, is a more practical look at PBL "Problem-Based Learn-ing: As Authentic as It Gets," by Stepien and Gallagher. The authors describe PBL in view of actual units used with students. In that con-text, they define problem-based learning and discuss different meth-ods of using it, ranging from fully unfolding units of study to "post-hole" techniques for short problems within a unit. Questions are emphasized as key to the process and staff development needs are also addressed in the article.

One other essay by Gallagher and Stepien, a seminal piece in the puzzle on PBL is "Content Acquisition in Problem-Based Learning: Depth Versus Breadth in American Studies." Based on the premise that many students will sacrifice knowledge of content when learning in nontraditional ways, such as PBL units, the authors make a con-vincing case for depth versus breadth in learning academic content, grounded in an American Studies class. Students are introduced to a messy situation, they are encouraged to take control of their learn-ing, and they are placed in the role of stakeholders in the problem. The resulting impact on the content learning as traditionally tested showed no significant differences in test scores between the tradi-tionally taught class and the PBL class. Some indications of teaching for depth vs breadth were supported, and the combination of process-based instruction with meaningful content was positively reported.

In a final essay, "Problem-Based Learning: An Instructional Model and Its Constructivist Framework," Savery and Duffy argue that "there's nothing so practical as good theory and there's nothing so theoretically interesting as good practice" (p. 31) in their discussion of constructivism and the teaching/learning process. They present evidence that PBL is predicated on the principles of constructivism and that the facilitation is focused on metacognitive processes of the students. In this way, the learner owns the problem and, in turn, that ownership drives the learning process.

With these five discussions providing a framework of understanding about the process and power of PBL, the remaining articles focus on practical applications for the classroom. As the reader delves into the specific applications, these initial discussions are often illuminated by example.

On Teaching for Understanding: A Conversation With Howard Gardner

by Ron Brandt

W *ould you say that most students don't really understand most of what they've been taught?*

I'm afraid they don't. All the evidence I can find suggests that's the case. Most schools have fallen into a pattern of giving kids exercises and drills that result in their getting answers on tests that look like understanding. It's what I call the "correct answer compromise": students read a text, they take a test, and everybody agrees that if they say a certain thing it'll be counted as understanding.

But the findings of cognitive research over the past 20–30 years are really quite compelling: students do not *understand,* in the most basic sense of that term. That is, they lack the capacity to take knowledge learned in one setting and apply it appropriately in a different setting. Study after Study has found that, by and large, even the best students in the best schools can't do that.

Could you give a couple of examples?

Okay. The most dramatic examples come from the physical sciences. Consider kids who get A's in physics courses in good high schools and colleges, who answer all the questions correctly on tests. If they're put in a situation outside of class and asked to explain what's going to happen—to draw a diagram, to make a prediction—they can't give the right answer; in fact, the answers they give tend to be

Brandt, R. (April 1993). "On Teaching for Understanding: A Conversation With Howard Gardner." *Educational Leadership* 50, 7: 4–7. Reprinted with permission of the Association for Supervision and Curriculum Development. Copyright © 1993 by ASCD. All rights reserved.

the same kinds of answers you'd get from 5-year-olds, the kinds of explanations that were given in Aristotle's time.

For example, you toss a coin in the air and ask these A students what's happening. They say, "Well, there's a certain force in my hand that I'm giving to the coin and the coin has it for a while and then the coin gets exhausted and just flops to the ground." In fact, as soon as the coin leaves your hand, the only force working on it is gravity, which ultimately pulls it down. But that's a nonintuitive, Newtonian explanation. Kids will give you that kind of explanation if they're asked for it on a test—but if they're asked about it on the street, they'll answer the way 5-year-olds do.

There's a famous example of Harvard Graduates being asked, as they received their diploma, why the earth is warmer in the summer than in the winter. Out of 25 students, nearly all gave exactly the same answer that a 5-year-old would: the earth is closer to the sun in summer than in the winter. The fact is, it has nothing to do with that; it has to do with the tilt of the earth on its axis, which is either away or toward the sun, depending on what time of the year it is in a particular location.

The research literature on "misconceptions" is pretty much restricted to science, isn't it?

I thought so, but in fact it turns up wherever you look—although the way it plays out is different. In mathematics, the problem is that kids learn formulas by rote, and they learn to plug numbers into those formulas. As long as the problem is presented with the items in the right order, so to speak, everything is all right. But as soon as the problem is given another way requiring the students to understand what the formula refers to, to be able to use it flexibly, then the students fail.

In the social sciences, the problems are stereotypes and what I call "scripts"; that is, we learn a certain way of thinking about things when we're very young. These are very powerful stories, and they're very long-lived. They influence the way we understand and explain things. For example, there's the Star Wars script: the good guys look like you, the bad guys look different, the two gangs struggle, and in the end, the good guys win.

In literature, there's a wonderful example from I. A. Richards, the great literary critic. In *Practical Criticism,* he reported asking

Cambridge University undergraduates, who ought to be pretty well qualified, to read some poems and tell what they meant and whether they were any good. But he didn't give them the names of the poets—and without that information, the students had no idea which poems were good and which were bad.

> I think that humans have evolved to the point that 5-year-olds can figure out most things they need to know to survive.

They rejected John Donne and accepted poets who couldn't get published in the local newspapers. These students, too, forgot what they supposedly had learned in poetry class and fell back to the aesthetics of a 5-year-old.

Speaking of 5-year-olds, in your book The Unschooled Mind *(1991), you give a lot of attention to the research on the learning of very young children. Why?*

I think that humans have evolved to the point that 5-year-olds can figure out most things they need to know to survive. When I was writing my book, I happened to have a 5-year-old (my son Benjamin), so I didn't have a problem finding a subject for my research. And by and large when I asked him questions, he gave answers as good as anybody who wasn't an expert. He was able to understand a point, able to think about things, even to evaluate alternatives. He could come up with metaphors, examples, and so on.

So a 5-year-old mind is a terrific invention! It has theories: theories of mind, theories of matter, theories of life, theories of self.

That's the good news. On the other hand, the 5-year-old also develops many notions that are just wrong. For example, you have a heavy object in your hand and a light object in your hand. You drop them both at the same time, and the heavy one falls quicker. It's a very appealing idea—but it's dead wrong.

There's the Star Wars script I talked about: people who look like you are good; people who look different from you are bad. You can see why, over the course of evolution, that was a pretty smart story to align yourself with. But it leads to all kinds of prejudices and biases.

So you might say that the challenge of education is, on the one hand, to preserve the imagination and the questioning and the theoretical stance of a 5-year-old, but on the other hand—gradually but decisively—to replace those ideas that are not well-founded with theories, ideas, conceptions, stories, which are more accurate.

BUT THAT DOESN'T ALWAYS HAPPEN.

Unfortunately, it seldom happens. As I argue in *The Unschooled Mind,* there are these engravings in the mind that are established early in life, and most of us never get rid of them. What school does is kind of pour powder over them so you can't see them. It makes kids look as if they have sophisticated understanding. But when the kids leave school, the understanding disappears, and the initial engravings are still there.

> **... there are powerful lessons to be learned from observing a good apprenticeship or a good children's museum.**

What can be done about it?

The best thing schools can do is come up with long-term regular procedures that gradually wear down those early engravings and that slowly construct better ones; more comprehensive theories, better explanations, less prejudiced views of the world.

In your book you suggest two models that could help schools make learning more authentic: children's museum-type programs and apprenticeships. Why those?

I was searching for learning situations that minimize the kind of mindless, context-less learning that takes place in schools and maximize people's understanding of why they're doing things—by giving them opportunities to try things out in new ways. And I came up with these institutions, one that's very old and one that's very new.

Now, people sometimes misinterpret my idea of apprenticeships to mean that I'm recommending seven-year signed contracts calling for kids to start out by sweeping the floor. With children's museums, they think I mean to close the schools and build a center with a reflecting pool in the middle. That's not what I mean at all.

What I do mean is that there are powerful lessons to be learned from observing a good apprenticeship or a good children's museum. In an apprenticeship, you see a young person hanging around a very knowledgeable adult—an expert, someone who really knows what he or she is doing—watching that person, day after day, as he uses his knowledge. The master challenges his apprentice at the level the apprentice can handle. He doesn't give her something she could do six months ago; he doesn't give her tasks that are way too difficult.

He's always calibrating the challenge for about where the student is. And I think that if you hang around an expert, not only will you develop requisite skills, you'll know when to use them and when not to use them.

But the point is for teachers and parents to think of themselves as masters and to challenge their apprentices. If the parent watches TV instead of reading, or the teacher reads one book a year—I'm told that's what the average teacher reads—that's the message the kids will get. But if the adults read and write and talk about current events, the kids will do it, too.

And children's museums?

Well, they're a very new invention. Ann Lewin, the head of the Capitol Children's Museum in Washington, D. C., calls them a new art form. They've grown dramatically in the last 25 years; there were just a handful in 1950–60, and now there are hundreds of them. They are places where kids can find things that interest them and explore these things at their own pace and in their own way. Frank Oppenheimer, who founded the Exploratorium in San Francisco said, "Nobody flunks museums."

A good museum is a child-friendly place to learn. And many people, including me, have been fascinated as we've escorted kids whom we thought we knew to children's museums and discovered unexpected strengths or unexpected areas of confusion. Or discover that kids we thought of as being unable to learn were terrific learners, but in a very different type of environment. It broadens your notion of what kids are like, and what they can do.

Of course, most teachers and principals don't have the resources, perhaps even the authority, to set up children's museum-like situations or establish apprenticeships.

Don't fall into that trap. The apprentice-master relationship is primarily a way of thinking. The master teacher thinks, "I'm not just passing on the contents of a textbook; I'm modeling a certain kind of knowledge and standards for making use of that knowledge in daily life." If you think of yourself like that, that's a revolutionary difference—and it doesn't cost a dime.

As for children's museums, many communities now have one. And I can't believe there's any regulation that precludes some commerce back and forth between the children's museum—its materials and its personnel— and the schools. The problem is that it's considered a frill rather than an important means of education.

> And the important thing is it doesn't matter the first or the second time they do something whether they have any idea as to what the "right" physical principle is . . .

And even in communities that don't have a children's museum, educators can visit one in another city and watch what's going on, see how kids interact with stuff, observe the learning. I recommend that teachers visiting the San Jose discovery Museum pretend to be 5-year-olds; regress to that age and see what it's like to learn about the world in those ways.

Why is that so important? What about the way things are done in children's museums makes for authentic learning?

Well, take the Exploratorium in San Francisco. First of all, it's put together by people who know a lot about science. It's designed to reflect scientific knowledge that has been developed in the past couple of centuries—but there's nothing didactic or intimidating there at all.

Instead, there are the actual experiments that lead people to draw conclusions about science. So the kids themselves have the chance to be little scientists, to try experiments and see what happens. And the important thing is it doesn't matter the first or the second time they do something whether they have any idea as to what the "right" physical principle is; they're getting familiar with the phenomena in a way that fits their own tempo, learning style, profile of intelligences. They're getting a chance to test some of their own intuitive notions and see what about them is tenable and what is inadequate.

And if they spend more time there, they can read some of the material the museum provides or they can talk with one of the explainers who come around, or hang around with a teacher or parent who knows some things. So in that realistic environment they can enter into a discussion about the meaning of the things people have discovered in the sciences or the arts.

When you've encountered an idea in your own way and brought your own thinking to a bear, the idea becomes much more a part of you. It isn't something that you read about from 3 o'clock to 3:15 and then forget; it's a part of your own experience. And if you're encouraged to take the lessons you learned in the Exploration and bring them home to your basement or your own room, or bring them to school—to what's going on in science class or art class—you then have what I call "resonance." The notion of resonance is that people are more likely to master concepts and understand potential implications of phenomena when they encounter them in difference places. Children who have made bubbles or played with pendulums in children's museums will understand them more fully when they encounter them at school.

Let me ask, then, how these principles apply to what teachers do day-by-day with the kids in their classrooms?

The first question the teacher should ask is, "Why am I doing this? Do I believe it's important? Can I convey that to kids?" Not just because it's the next lesson, or because it comes from the textbook.

Then, the teachers need to figure out what's the very best way to introduce kids to this phenomenon: what's the generative idea, the puzzle, the thing that's really going to compel, maybe because it's surprising or intriguing.

Then it's important to provide what I call "multiple entry points." Kids don't all learn in the same way; they don't all find the same things interesting. In fact, based on my theory of multiple intelligences introduced in *Frames of Mind*,[1] I'd say that you can approach almost any rich topic in a whole variety of ways.

We need to give kids a chance in school to enter the room by different windows, so to speak—but to be able to see the relationships among different types of windows.

Another obvious implication, one that only a few people have begun to take seriously, is that we've got to do a lot fewer things in school. The greatest enemy of understanding is coverage. As long as you are determined to cover everything, you actually ensure that most kids are not going to understand. You've got to take enough time to get kids deeply involved in something so they can think about it in lots of different ways and apply it—not just at school but at home and on the street and so on.

[handwritten margin note: Read aloud w/ PBL]

Now, this is the most revolutionary idea in American education—because most people can't abide the notion that we might leave out one decade of American history or one formula in math or one biological system. But that's crazy, because we now know that kids don't understand those things anyway. They forget them a soon as the test is over—because it hasn't been built into their brain, engraved in it. So since we know unambiguously that the way we do it now isn't working, we have to try something else.

You're really convinced of that?

Let me give you an example. Having written *The Unschooled Mind* and thinking that the ideas had a certain power, I tried out the theories on my graduate students studying cognitive development. At the beginning of the year, the middle of the year, the end of the year, I gave all the students two tests. One was a conventional test of content knowledge: who was Piaget, what his theories were about; things like that. But the other was a test of understanding. I would give the students new situations that they hadn't seen before—articles out of the newspaper or phenomena that I just made up—and I would ask them to explain those phenomena.

> **Over the course of the term, the students' mastery of content zoomed up.**

Well, the results were very striking. Over the course of the term, the students' mastery of content zoomed up. Their understandings, on the other hand, were exactly the same; they didn't change at all. How humiliating! I could just see the headlines, "Harvard Professor of Well-Regarded Courses Documents That His Own Students Don't Understand."

Fortunately, it's a two-year program, so we're rewriting the course now; we're going to teach it very differently. So the message, I guess, is "Physician, heal thyself."

Editor's Note: As a service to our members, ASCD has arranged to distribute Howard Gardner's *The Unschooled Mind*, (1991), (New York: Basic Books). It is available from ASCD for $23, Stock #511-05393.

NOTES

1. H. Gardner, (1983), *Frames of Mind,* 10th Anniversary Edition. 1993. (New York: Basic Books).

Five Standards of Authentic Instruction

by Fred M. Newmann and Gary G. Wehlage

> What types of instruction engage students in using their minds well?
> A framework developed at Wisconsin's Center on Organization and
> Restructuring of Schools may be a valuable tool for teachers and
> researchers attempting to answer this complex question.

W hy do many innovations fail to improve the quality of
instruction or student achievement? In 1990, we began to
explore this question by studying schools that have tried to
restructure. Unfortunately, even the most innovative activities—
from school councils and shared decision making to cooperative
learning and assessment by portfolio—can be implemented in ways
that undermine meaningful learning, unless they are guided by substantive, worthwhile educational ends. We contend that innovations
should aim toward a vision of authentic student achievement, and
we are examining the extent to which instruction in restructured
schools is directed toward authentic forms of student achievement.
We use the word *authentic* to distinguish between achievement that
is significant and meaningful and that which is trivial and useless.

To define authentic achievement more precisely, we rely on
three criteria that are consistent with major proposals in the restructuring movement:[1] (1) students construct meaning and produce
knowledge, (2) students use disciplined inquiry to construct meaning, and (3) students aim their work toward production of discourse,
products, and performances that have value or meaning beyond
success in school.[2]

THE NEED FOR STANDARDS FOR INSTRUCTION

While there has been much recent attention to standards for curriculum and for assessment,[3] public and professional discussion of standards for instruction tends to focus on procedural and technical aspects, with little attention to more fundamental standards of quality. Is achievement more likely to be authentic when the length of class periods varies, when teachers teach in teams, when students participate in hands-on activities, or when students spend time in cooperative groups, museums, or on-the-job apprenticeships?

We were cautious not to assume that technical processes or specific sites for learning, however innovative, necessarily produce experiences of high intellectual quality. Even activities that place students in the role of a more active, cooperative learner and that seem to respect student voices can be implemented in ways that do not produce authentic achievement. The challenge is not simply to adopt innovative teaching techniques or to find new locations for learning, but deliberately to counteract two persistent maladies that make conventional schooling inauthentic:

1.   Often the work students do does not allow them to use their minds well.

2.   The work has no intrinsic meaning or value to students beyond achieving success in school.

To face these problems head-on, we articulated standards for instruction that represented the quality of intellectual work but that were not tied to any specific learning activity (for example, lecture or small-group discussion). Indeed, the point was to assess the extent to which any given activity—traditional or innovative, in or out of school—engages students in using their minds well.

Instruction is complex, and quantification in education can often be as misleading as informative. To guard against oversimplification, we formulated several standards, rather than only one or two, and we conceptualized each standard as a continuous construct from "less" to "more" of a quality, rather than as a categorical (yes or no) variable. We expressed each standard as a dimensional construct on a five-point scale. Instructions for rating lessons include specific criteria for each score—1 to 5—on each standard. Space does not permit us to present criteria for some specific ratings. Raters consider both the number of students to which the criterion applies and the proportion of class time during which it applies.[4] The five standards are: higher-order thinking, depth of knowledge, connectedness to the world beyond the classroom, substantive conversation, and social support for student achievement (see fig. 1).

Figure 1
Five Standards of Authentic Instruction
1. Higher-Order Thinking
lower-order thinking only 1...2...3...4...5 higher-order thinking is central

2. Depth of Knowledge
knowledge is shallow 1...2...3...4...5 knowledge is deep

3. Connectedness to the World Beyond the Classroom
no connection 1...2...3...4...5 connected

4. Substantive Conversation
no substantive conversation 1...2...3...4...5 high-level substantive conversation

5. Social Support for Student Achievement
negative social support 1...2...3...4...5 positive social support

---

HIGHER-ORDER THINKING

The first scale measures the degree to which students use higher-order thinking.

Lower-order thinking (LOT) occurs when students are asked to receive or recite factual information or to employ rules and algorithms through repetitive routines. As information-receivers, students are given pre-specified knowledge ranging from simple facts and information to more complex concepts. Students are in this role when they recite previously acquired knowledge by responding to questions that require recall of pre-specified knowledge.

Higher-order thinking (HOT) requires students to manipulate information and ideas in ways that transform their meaning and implications, such as when students combine facts and ideas in order to synthesize, generalize, explain, hypothesize, or arrive at some conclusion or interpretation. Manipulating information and ideas through these processes allows students to solve problems and discover new (for them) meanings and understandings. When students engage in HOT, an element of uncertainty is introduced, and instructional outcomes are not always predictable.

Criteria for higher-order thinking:
3 = Students primarily engage in routine LOT operations a good share of the lesson. There is at least one significant question or activity in which some students perform some HOT operations.
4 = Students engage in an at least one major activity during the lesson in which they perform HOT operations. This activity occupies a substantial portion of the lesson, and many students perform HOT.

DEPTH OF KNOWLEDGE

From "knowledge is shallow" (1) to "knowledge is deep" (5), the next scale assesses students' depth of knowledge and understanding. This term refers to the substantive character of the ideas in a lesson and to the level of understanding that students demonstrate as they consider these ideas.

Knowledge is thin or superficial when it does not deal with significant concepts of a topic or discipline—for example, when students have a trivial understanding of important concepts or when they have only a surface acquaintance with their meaning. Superficiality can be due, in part, to instructional strategies that emphasize coverage of large quantities of fragmented information.

Knowledge is deep or thick when it concerns the central ideas of a topic or discipline. For students, knowledge is deep when they make clear distinctions, develop arguments, solve problems, construct explanations, and otherwise work with relatively complex understandings. Depth is produced, in part, by covering fewer topics in systematic and connected ways.

Criteria for depth of knowledge:
2 = Knowledge remains superficial and fragmented; while some key concepts and ideas are mentioned or covered, only a superficial acquaintance or trivialized understanding of these complex ideas is evident.
3 = Knowledge is treated unevenly during instruction; that is, deep understanding of something is countered by superficial understanding of other ideas. At least one significant idea may be presented in depth and its significance grasped, but in general the focus is not sustained.

CONNECTEDNESS TO THE WORLD

The third scale measures the extent to which the class has value and meaning beyond the instructional context. In a class with little or no value beyond, activities are deemed important for success only in school (now or later). Students' work has no impact on others and serves only to certify their level of compliance with the norms of formal schooling.

A lesson gains in authenticity the more there is a connection to the larger social context within which students live. Instruction can exhibit some degree of connectedness when (1) students address real-world public problems (for example, clarifying a contemporary issue by applying statistical analysis in a report to the city council on the homeless); or (2) students use personal experiences as a context for applying knowledge (such as using conflict resolution techniques in their own school).

> **Criteria for connectedness:**
> 1 = Lesson topic and activities have no clear connection to issues or experience beyond the classroom. The teacher offers no justification for the work beyond the need to perform well in class.
> 5 = Students work on a problem or issue that the teacher and students see as connected to their personal experiences or contemporary public situations. They explore these connections in ways that create personal meaning. Students are involved in an effort to influence an audience beyond their classroom; for example, by communicating knowledge to others, advocating solutions to social problems, providing assistance to people, or creating performances or products with utilitarian or aesthetic value.

SUBSTANTIVE CONVERSATION

From "no substantive conversation" (1) to "high-level substantive conversation" (5), the fourth scale accesses the extent of talking to learn and understand the substance of a subject. In classes with little or no substantive conversation, interaction typically consists of a lecture with recitation in which the teacher deviates very little from delivering a preplanned body of information and set of questions; students routinely give very short answers. Teachers' list of questions, facts, and concepts tend to make the discourse choppy, rather than coherent; there is often little or no follow-up of student responses. Such discourse is the oral equivalent of fill-in-the-blank or short-answer study questions.

High levels of substantive conversation are indicated by three features:

1. There is considerable interaction about the ideas of a topic (the talk is about disciplined subject matter and includes indicators of higher-order thinking such as making distinctions, applying ideas, forming generalizations, raising questions, and not just reporting experiences, facts, definitions, or procedures).

2. Sharing of ideas is evident in exchanges that are not completely scripted or controlled (as in a teacher-led recitation). Sharing is best illustrated when participants explain themselves or ask questions in complete sentences and when they respond directly to comments of previous speakers.

3. The dialogue builds coherently on participants' ideas to promote improved collective understanding of a theme or topic.

> **Criteria for substantive conversation:**
> To score 2 or above, conversation must focus on subject matter as in feature (1) above.
> 2 = Sharing (2) and/or coherent promotion of collective understanding (3) occurs briefly and involves at least one example of two consecutive interchanges.
> 4 = All three features of substantive conversation occur, with at least one example of sustained conversation (that is, at least three consecutive interchanges), and many students participate.

SOCIAL SUPPORT FOR STUDENT ACHIEVEMENT

The social support scale involves high expectations, respect, and inclusion of all students in the learning process. Social support is low when teacher or student behavior, comments, and actions tend to discourage effort, participation, or willingness to express one's views. Support can also be low if no overt acts like the above occur, but when the overall atmosphere of the class is negative as a result of previous behavior. Token acknowledgments, even praise, by the teacher of student actions or responses do not necessarily constitute evidence of social support.

Social support is high in classes when the teacher conveys high expectations for all students, including that it is necessary to take risks and try hard to master challenging academic work, that all members of the class can learn important knowledge and skills, and that a climate of mutual respect among all members of the class contributes to achievement by all. "Mutual respect" means that students with less skill or proficiency in a subject are treated in ways that encourage their efforts and value their contributions.

> **Criteria for social support:**
> 2 = Social support is mixed. Both negative and positive behaviors or comments are observed.
> 5 = Social support is strong. The class is characterized by high expectations, challenging work, strong effort, mutual respect, and assistance in achievement for almost all students. Both teacher and students demonstrate a number of these attitudes by soliciting and welcoming contributions from all students. Broad student participation may indicate that low-achieving students receive social support for learning.

USING THE FRAMEWORK TO OBSERVE INSTRUCTION

We are now using the five standards to estimate levels of authentic instruction in social studies and mathematics in elementary, middle, and high schools that have restructured in various ways. Our purpose is not to evaluate schools or teachers, but to learn how authentic instruction and student achievement are facilitated or impeded by:

• organizational features of schools (teacher workload, scheduling of instruction, governance structure);

• the content of particular programs aimed at curriculum, assessment, or staff development;

• the quality of school leadership;

• school and community culture.

We are also examining how actions of districts, states, and regional or national reform projects influence instruction. The findings will describe the conditions under which "restructuring" improves instruction for students and suggest implications for policy and practice.

Apart from its value as a research tool, the framework should also help teachers reflect upon their teaching. The framework provides a set of standards through which to view assignments, instructional activities, and the dialogue between teacher and students and students with one another. Teachers, either alone or with peers, can use the framework to generate questions, clarify goals, and critique their teaching. For example, students may seem more engaged in activities such as cooperative learning or long-term projects, but heightened participation alone is not sufficient. The standards provide further criteria for examining the extent to which such activities actually put students' minds to work on authentic questions.

In using the framework, either for reflective critiques of teaching or for research, it is important to recognize its limitations. First, the framework does not try to capture in an exhaustive way all that teachers may be trying to accomplish with students. The standards attempt only to represent in a quantitative sense the degree of authentic instruction observed within discrete class periods. Numerical ratings alone cannot portray how lessons relate to one another or how multiple lessons might accumulate into experiences more complex than the sum of individual lessons. Second, the relative importance of the different standards remains open for discussion. Each suggests a distinct ideal, but it is probably not possible for most teachers to show high performance on all standards in most of their lessons. Instead, it may be important to ask, "Which standards should receive higher priority and under what circumstances?"[5]

> ... "Which standards should receive higher priority and under what circumstances?"

Finally, although previous research indicates that teaching for thinking, problem solving, and understanding often has more positive effects on student achievement than traditional teaching, the effects of this specific framework for authentic instruction on student achievement have not been examined.[6] Many educators insist that there are appropriate times for traditional, less authentic instruction—emphasizing memorization, repetitive practice, silent study without conversation, and brief exposure—as well as teaching for in-depth understanding.

Rather than choosing rigidly and exclusively between traditional and authentic forms of instruction, it seems more reasonable to focus on how to move instruction toward more authentic accomplishments for students. Without promising to resolve all the dilemmas faced by thoughtful teachers, we hope the standards will offer some help in this venture.

Authors' Note: This paper was prepared at the Center on Organization and Restructuring of Schools, supported by the U. S. Department of Education, Office of Educational Research and Improvement (Grant No. R117Q0005-92) and by the Wisconsin

Center of Education Research, School of Education, University of Wisconsin–Madison. Major contributions to the development of these standards have been made by Center staff members. The opinions expressed here are those of the authors and do not necessarily reflect the views of the supporting agencies.

NOTES

1. See Carnegie Corporation of New York (1989), Elmore and Associates (1990), and Murphy (1991).

2. See Archbald and Newmann 1988, Newmann 1991, Newmann and Archbald 1992, Newmann et al. 1992, and Wehlage et al. 1989.

3. For example, see the arguments for standards in National Council on Education Standards and Testing (1992), and Smith and O'Day (1991).

4. In three semesters of data collection, correlations between raters were .7 or higher, and precise agreement between raters was about 60 percent or higher for each of the dimensions. A detailed scoring manual will be available to the public following completion of data collection in 1994.

5. The standards may be conceptually distinct, but initial findings indicate that they cluster together statistically as a single construct. That is, lessons rated high or low on some dimensions tend to be rated in the same direction on others.

6. Evidence for positive achievement effects of teaching for thinking is provided in diverse sources such as Brown and Palincsar (1989), Carpenter and Fennema (1992), Knapp et al. (1992), and Resnick (1987). However, no significant body of research to date has clarified key dimensions of instruction that produce *authentic* forms of student achievement as defined here.

REFERENCES

Archbald, D., and F. M. Newmann. (1988). *Beyond Standardized Testing: Assessing Authentic Academic Achievement in the Secondary School.* Reston, Va.: National Association of Secondary School Principals.

Brown, A., and A. Palincsar. (March 1989). "Coherence and Causality in Science Readings." Paper presented at the annual meeting of the American Educational Research Association, San Francisco.

Carnegie Corporation of New York. (1989). *Turning Points: Preparing American Youth for the 21st Century.* Report on the Carnegie Task Force on the Education of Young Adolescents. New York: Carnegie Council on Adolescent Development.

Carpenter, T. P., and E. Fennema. (1992). "Cognitively Guided Instruction: Building on the Knowledge of Students and Teachers." In *Curriculum Reform: The Case of Mathematics in the United States.* Special issue of *International Journal of Educational Research,* edited by W. Secada, pp. 457–470. Elmsford, N.Y.: Pergamon Press, Inc.

Elmore, R. F., and Associates. (1990). *Restructuring Schools: The Next Generation of Educational Reform.* San Francisco: Jossey-Bass.

Knapp, M. S., P. M. Shields, and B. J. Turnbull. (1992). *Academic Challenge for the Children of Poverty: Summary Report.* Washington, D. C.: U. S. Department of Education, Office of Policy and Planning.

Murphy, J. (1991). *Restructuring Schools: Capturing and Assessing the Phenomena.* Nashville, Tenn.: National Center for Educational Leadership, Vanderbilt University.

National Council on Education Standards and Testing. (1992). *Raising Standards for American Education.* A Report to Congress, the Secretary of Education, the National Education Goals Panel, and the American People, Washington, D.C.: U. S. Government Printing Office, Superintendent of Documents, Mail Stop SSOP.

Newmann, F. M. (1991). "Linking Restructuring to Authentic Student Achievement." *Phi Delta Kappan 72,* 6: 458–463.

Newmann, F. M., and D. Archbald. (1992). "The Nature of Authentic Academic Achievement." In *Toward a New Science of Educational Testing and Assessment,* edited by H. Berlak, F. M. Newmann, E. Adams, D. A. Archbald, T. Burgess, J. Raven, and T. A. Romberg, pp. 71–84. Albany, N.Y.: SUNY Press.

Newmann, F. M., G. G. Wehlage, and S. D. Lamborn. (1992). "The Significance and Sources of Student Engagement." In *Student Engagement and Achievement in American Secondary Schools,* edited by F. M. Newmann, pp. 11–30. New York: Teachers College Press.

Resnick, L. (1987). *Education and Learning to Think.* Washington, D. C.: National Academy Press.

Smith, M. S., and J. O'Day. (1991). "Systemic School Reform." In *The Politics of Curriculum and Testing: The 1990 Yearbook of the Politics of Education Association,* edited by S. H. Fuhrman and B. Malen, pp. 233–267. Philadelphia: Falmer Press.

Wehlage, G. G., R. A. Rutter, G. A. Smith, N. Lesko, and R. R. Fernandez. (1989). *Reducing the Risk: Schools as Communities of Support.* Philadelphia: Falmer Press.

Problem-Based Learning: As Authentic as It Gets

by William Stepien and Shelagh Gallagher

An innovative high school is pioneering ways to engage students in solving problems by having them take on the roles of scientists, doctors, artists, and historians. In addition, the Center for Problem-Based Learning is helping other educators learn these exciting techniques.

L ast summer 100 7th and 8th grade students got off buses in front of a chain-link fence where a nuclear warning sign was posted. In front of them was a grass-covered hill where thousands of cubic feet of thorium are buried. They were there to solve the "thorium waste problem."

As part of a week-long Illinois Mathematics and Science Academy (IMSA) summer program, the students were taking the roles of scientists working for the Illinois Nuclear Regulatory Commission. After visiting the West Chicago site, surveying the community, and conducting experiments, they presented their solutions to state government experts, scientists, and community activists.

Not that the "thorium problem" is an easy problem to solve. On the contrary, it is an authentic problem and one fraught with controversy. Scientists do not agree about the health risks posed by the low-level nuclear materials. Activists want all the material moved somewhere else even if the solution bankrupts the company. And some members of the Illinois General Assembly want the thorium removed from the state even though there is no place in the country currently licensed to accept the material. The company believes entombing the thorium at the site is the best solution.

Stepien W., Gallagher, S. (April 1993). "Problem-Based Learning: As Authentic as it Gets." *Educational Leadership* 50, 7: 25–28. Reprinted with permission of the Association for Supervision and Curriculum Development. Copyright © 1993 by ASCD. All rights reserved.

This is just one of the problem-based learning (PBL) units designed by the staffs at the Center for Problem-Based Learning and IMSA to increase students' achievement and motivation. Through problem-based learning, students learn how to use an iterative process of assessing what they know, identifying what they need to know, gathering information, and collaborating on the evaluation of hypotheses in light of the data they have collected. Their teachers act as coaches and tutors: probing findings, hypotheses, and conclusions; sharing their thinking when students need a model; and attending to metacognitive growth by way of "time out" discussions on how thinking is progressing.

> Through problem-based learning, students learn how to use an iterative process of assessing what they know, identifying what they need to know, gathering information, and collaborating on the evaluation . . .

These investigations of the connectedness and complexity of real-world problems nurture collaboration among learners, provide instructional tasks appropriately challenging for the targeted students, and promote performance assessments based upon the context of each learning situation.

WHAT IS PROBLEM-BASED LEARNING?

Problem-based learning turns instruction topsy-turvy. Students meet an "ill-structured problem" before they receive any instruction. In the place of covering the curriculum, learners probe deeply into issues searching for connections, grappling with complexity, and using knowledge to fashion solutions. As with real problems, students encountering ill-structured problems will not have most of the relevant information needed to solve the problem at the outset. Nor will they know exactly what actions are required for resolution. After they tackle the problem, the definition of the problem may change. And even after they propose a solution, the students will never be sure they have made the right decision. They will have had the experience of having to make the best possible decision based on the information at hand.

They will also have had a stake in the problem. In problem-based learning students assume the roles of scientists, historians, doctors, or others who have a real stake in the proposed problem.

Motivation soars because students realize it's their problem. By having a stake, they come to realize that no real-world problem is objective, that every point of view comes with a bias toward interpreting data in a certain way.

Teachers take on new roles in problem-based learning, too. First they act as models, thinking aloud with students and practicing behavior they want their students to use. They familiarize students with metacognitive questions such as, What's going on here? What do we need to know more about? What did we do during the problem that was effective? Then they coax and prompt students to use the questions and take on the responsibility for the problem. As time goes on, students become self-directed learners. To encourage the students' independence, the teachers then fade into the background and assume the role of colleagues on the problem-solving team.

> In the process of problem-solving, students crisscross a variety of disciplines.

In the process of problem solving, students crisscross a variety of disciplines. They build substantial knowledge bases through increasingly self-directed study. Through collaboration with their classmates, students refine and enlarge their new knowledge in long-term memory in such a way to promote transfer to new problems. As they move toward solutions, they identify conflicting ethical appeals. And when it is time for resolution, they present, justify, and debate solutions, looking for the "best fit." Problem-based learning is apprenticeship for real-life problem solving.

INNOVATIVE PROGRAMS FOR PROBLEM-BASED LEARNING

Over the last three years, the Center for Problem-Based Learning at IMSA has been developing innovative programs incorporating problem-based learning into a variety of K–12 settings. As a research and development facility, the Center uses IMSA as a testing ground and also offers its services through partnership with other schools and institutions. Some special programs are funded by various private sector grants, including corporate and foundation donors.

One course developed at IMSA called Science, Society, and the Future is a semester-long elective for seniors that focuses on unresolved science-related social issues. The course is interdisciplinary and taught by a team of teachers, one from science and one from the social sciences. Students learn *exclusively* through the use of ill-structured problems.

One activity has seniors pondering patient files, searching for the cause of pneumonia contracted by 22 residents of a community of 20,000. Taking the roles of public health officials, they will soon discover the chilling fact that the bacterium *L. pneumonphilia* (Legionnaires' disease) has been found in the lungs of one of the patients. They will need to ask: What does this new information do to the problem? What is this agent like? What does it do to its hosts?

At the end of another week of investigation, the seniors are highly suspicious that a misting system in the produce section of a local supermarket may be the source of the outbreak. They have set time aside to talk about the situation with the school's biology teachers. Some of the students are consulting the state statutes for clues about the powers they can exert as public health officials. A third group is getting ready for a press conference where they will meet reporters concerned about how long it has taken for the officials to track down the source.

"POST-HOLE" PROBLEMS

Another way teachers use problem-based learning is though "post-holes." Post-holes are short problems that can be used when teachers don't want to design their entire course around problems but do want to induce one occasionally. For instance, in a course in German, third-year students arrive in class one day to find a letter from the Nazi Ministry of Propaganda (written in German since all IMSA language classes use immersion). The letter, dated 1938, addresses the students as "Gallery Directors" who must review their art collection and discard that which is degenerate. Degenerate art will no longer be tolerated in Germany. The gallery owners—the students—face severe sanctions if they do not weed out paintings, statues, and photographs that are contrary to the vision and purpose of art held by the government officials. The German teacher asks his students: *"Was mussen wir wissen?" (What must we know?)*

As the situation unfolds, the gallery owners share what they know about the Nazis but soon recognize that they need to know much more. The teacher mentions sources they can consult about the philosophy of the Nazi movement. IMSA's art teacher visits the gallery to talk about the works of art. Students must then evaluate the entire collection of 20 pieces, each depicted on a separate 35 mm slide.

Based upon research into the events of the late 1930s in Germany, the students judge that 10 pieces in the collection might actually be considered degenerate. Now they must ask: What should we do about the 10 items? What penalties might we face if we do not remove them? Is it right for the government to demand this? Is there any way to negotiate with the Nazis? Are the items worth saving in the face of the risk to us?

THE QUESTIONS ARE KEY

Teachers help students organize their thinking through problem-based learning. For instance, in American Studies, IMSA sophomores in the role of Directors of the Virginia colony are requested to explain to the King what they are going to do about the fact that colonial Virginia has not produced revenue for the last three years. Under a heading of "What do we know?" on the chalkboard, the students begin to list facts about the settlement of Virginia recalled from previous contact with American history. Not much help here! The teacher starts a new section: "What do we need to know?" The board begins to fill up quickly: Don't we have a charter with the King? What did we promise? What do we get from the Crown in return? Are there other colonies in the New World? How well are they doing? What are they doing to make a profit? Is there contact with natives? What is the contact like? What is life in Virginia like?

> Teachers help students organize their thinking through problem-based learning.

As the questions are collected, the teacher prompts new lines of thought: "What are you thinking about? Have you got a hunch about something?" Hypotheses are written on a third section of the board. As the ideas are listed, the teacher probes for the type of information that will help the students decide whether a hypothesis is true, false, or needs refinement.

At the close of each class period, the students agree on which questions should be considered before the next class meeting. The assignment of questions is completed and students decide whether their textbooks or materials in the library are the best resources to consult.

After a few days, a second letter arrives in class. A member of the King's inner circle warns the directors that the King is becoming extremely concerned. The source suggests the directors must do something—and soon! The students must now use what they know, even if it is incomplete or contains conflicting data, to decide on the nature of their problem. After an acceptable problem statement has been crafted, the students turn their attention to solutions.

> After an acceptable problem statement has been crafted, the students turn their attention to solutions.

Assessment during PBL units takes place through the use of periodic exercises collected as a problem log. The exercises are designed to sample student thinking at different stages and to check on skill development related to information gathering, analysis, and evaluation. The final performance assessment in this American Studies unit involves package and careful review of a meeting between the King (another teacher) and three of the directors, chosen by lot. No test is given.

STAFF DEVELOPMENT NEEDED

Because the direct engagement of students in solving ill-structured problems requires a significant restructuring of what goes on in the classroom, the Center for Problem-Based Learning has begun to offer training in PBL at selected sites around the country. Each partnership involves introductory training of participating school personnel in tutorial teaching strategies and the design of problem-based units. Some partnerships include extensive curriculum development activity.

For example, a grant from the Jacob K. Javits Gifted and Talented Program allowed the Center for Gifted Education at The College of William and Mary to collaborate with teachers, scientists, and Center staff to develop science materials for elementary grades using problem-based learning. Each problem is designed to reveal something about the concept "systems" and uses content material often found in elementary school curriculum.

Social studies and science teachers at DeWitt Clinton High School in the Bronx, New York, are experimenting with the creation of PBL "post-holes" for their required courses. They are asking students with a wide range of abilities to work with ill-structured problems in world history, American history, government, and the sciences.

The Wall Street Journal's student edition offers a problem-based case study in each month's issue. Written as a two- or three-class period activity, each problem is created from an article that has recently appeared in the *Wall Street Journal.* The topics range from the spotted owl controversy to the plight of the mentally ill living in homeless shelters across America. A teacher's guide for each problem includes strategies for considering the conflicting ethical appeals in each problem.

With training and appropriate materials, problem-based learning becomes not simply a way to learn problem solving but a way to learn content and skills as well. The problem is the center of problem-based learning, and the learning is as authentic as learning can get!

Content Acquisition in Problem-Based Learning: Depth Versus Breadth in American Studies

by Shelagh A. Gallagher and William J. Stepien   (experts)

A continuing barrier to the implementation of curriculum fostering higher order thinking skills is the perception that use of these programs inevitably results in lower levels of content acquisition. This assumption was challenged in the current study, which compared high school students' scores on a multiple-choice standardized test after traditional or experimental instruction. Students in the experimental classroom were instructed by using an approach called problem-based learning where all ill-structured problem initiates learning and the teacher serves as a coach instead of an information repository. Results indicate that students in the experimental class did not sacrifice content acquisition when compared to students learning in more traditional settings. Implications regarding the breadth-versus-depth debate are discussed along with questions of research methodology in this area.

Very few people doubt the need to reform the way American history is taught to students. Trends reported in the National Assessment of Educational Progress (NAEP) provide a bleak picture of students' knowledge about history: in 1986 the average score on the 141–item NAEP history test was 54.5%; more recent reports show no improvement in this pattern (Patrick, 1991). Although some of this deficit can be attributed to the fact that 15% of American students are not required to take American history (Gagnon, 1989), clearly the problem goes deeper than enrollment. Even the students who are taking history are failing to absorb information about the foundations of our nation. Nor does the problem

From *Journal for the Education of the Gifted*, Vol. 19, No. 3, 1996, pp. 257–275.

end with fact-based literacy. The business community is making an increasingly loud call for change in education, requesting that students be trained to face the information age with skills in problem solving, critical inquiry, and information manipulation instead of factual recall (Committee for Economic Development, 1985; Rutherford & Ahlgren, 1990).

Inquiry in the Social Studies Curriculum. In response to the demands of a changing world, theoreticians and practitioners alike are calling for a restructured curriculum. Depending on their specific area of interest, they call for a curriculum that is thoughtful and provocative (Brown, 1991), for instruction that fosters higher order thinking and problem solving (Carter, 1988; Newmann, 1990), and instruction that focuses on depth of understanding instead of breadth of coverage (Wiggins, 1989). Recommendations from the Bradley Commission on History in the Schools (1989) reflect this advice, advocating a curriculum that is based on the assumption that:

> Study must reach well beyond the acquisition of useful information. To develop judgment and perspective, historical study must often focus upon broad, significant themes and questions, rather than the short-lived memorization of facts without context. In doing so, historical study should provide context for facts and training in critical judgment based upon evidence, including original sources, and should cultivate the perspective arising from a chronological view of the past down to the present day. (Gagnon, 1989, p. 23)

Among the disciplines, the social studies has consistently been in the forefront of curriculum development geared toward developing critical reasoning skills, generally through the medium of meaningful problems. Advocacy for a problem-oriented approach can be found as early as the 1916 report of the Committee of the Social Studies (NEA, 1916) to implement a senior-year course entitled "Problems of Democracy." A series of programs alternately called "problems approach" (Gross, 1989) or "issues-centered" (Evans, 1989) have followed. Hunt and Metcalf (1971) list the common goals that these curricula shared:

1.   Whenever one belief or conclusion is preferred to another, it is because the evidence, no matter how slight, is in its favor.

2.   Conclusions are provisional. All knowledge is relative and what we believe today may turn out tomorrow to be false. . . .

3. Conclusions have to be consistent with one another.

4. Although all the evidence can never be in, we rest our conclusions on the pertinent evidence known to us . . .

5. All operations must be performed openly and in a fashion that will make it possible for others to repeat our procedures. . . .

6. The authority for a conclusion is in perceivable phenomena. (p. 5)

Important examples of this movement are outlined by Parker (1991), who defines its progress around four seminal projects: (a) in the 1930s and 1940s, an attempt was made to implement a thinking curriculum based on interpreting the real meaning behind propaganda; (b) in the 1950s, the Harvard Social Studies Project looked at the curriculum through the analytical viewpoint of legalistic reasoning; (c) Taba (1962) also emphasized critical thinking, but in a discovery-oriented context and with a well-defined scheme of teacher questioning to guide the class; and (d) today, the Newmann Project integrates skill development and meaningful content to achieve the ultimate goal of complex thinking.

As the form and structure of these inquiry- and problem-oriented approaches developed, so did the research literature in cognitive psychology, documenting the benefits of learning in a complex environment. Instruction that fosters higher order thinking can result in learners who can construct meaningful connections between pieces of information (Voss, 1989), transfer information to new settings (Spiro, Feltovich, Coulson, & Anderson, 1989), and are motivated to learn (Knight & Waxman, 1991). Knowledge about problem solving has also expanded. Research now documents that problem-solving activities using realistic problems produce more creative responses than "generic" ill-structured problems and that problem finding predicts creativity better than more common psychometric measures (Okuda, Runco, & Berger, 1991). Problem solving using a real-world ill-structured problem also requires a different set of skills than "standard" problem solving. The amount of searching necessary (and by implication, the amount of learning) is increased when students are confronted by an ill-structured problem (Newell, 1980). An expanded range of questions must also be addressed in order to find a solution (Chand & Runco, 1993), again suggesting an expanded exposure to information.

Barriers to Reform in Social Studies Education. Unfortunately, even with all of the available arguments supporting a transition in both content and delivery of information, adaptation of curriculum and instruction classroom by classroom has been slow. Research by Onosko (1991) addressed the question of why traditional instruction still dominates the social studies classroom. Fifty-six teachers in 16 different social studies departments nationwide were asked to list the key barriers to changing their classroom practice. Among the most frequently mentioned barriers was the pressure—either external or self-imposed—for content coverage.

> Fifty-six teachers in 16 different social studies departments nationwide were asked to list the key barriers to changing their classroom practice.

Central to the argument against depth of understanding and in favor of breadth of content coverage is the assumption that students will learn less information if they are in a process-based classroom. It has become accepted that a focus on higher order thinking skills necessarily drives content out of the curriculum, leaving it devoid of meaningful information. Even those who admit to the advantages of gains in thinking skills are occasionally stymied by this supposed limitation, which overshadows the available documentation that problem-oriented approaches contribute to political socialization (Ehman, 1969), political awareness (Torney-Purta, 1986), and higher level thinking and moral reasoning (Taba, cited in Maker, 1982). After a review of several social studies curricula designed to foster critical thinking, VanSickle & Hoge (1991) concluded that, "In light of . . . the stress toward broad content coverage in middle and high school social studies courses, it might not be feasible to teach higher-cognitive skills in most social studies courses" (p. 169).

Despite a growing body of evidence that didactic lecture may not be as effective a delivery technique as it once seemed, the fear of losing content acquisition persists. Data questioning the efficacy of lecturing is gathering from two different venues. First, instruction based on information transmission fails to foster critical-thinking skills. Cognitive psychologists have demonstrated that instruction geared toward discrete pieces of information actually inhibits the use of higher order, flexible problem solving (Spiro, Vispoel, Schmitz, Samarapugavan, & Boerger, 1987). Conversely, process-oriented instruction may be related to enhanced achievement. In mathematics, process-oriented instruction was an indicator of higher NAEP scores (Mullis & Jenkins, 1988); and a study of science achievement has shown that process-oriented instruction in middle school was a positive predictor of later science achievement even when other predictors, such as prior achievement and parental education were taken into account (Gallagher, 1994). However, these studies are abstract; Girault's (1971) complaint that there is ". . . painful absence of hard research concerning the effectiveness of the problems approach in the social studies classroom" (p. 80) is still largely true today.

> . . . the Harvard Social Studies Project obtained results supporting higher order thinking as an avenue to factual learning . . .

In one of the few existing studies, the Harvard Social Studies Project obtained results supporting higher order thinking as an avenue to factual learning; equivalent levels of content acquisition were found among students in problem-centered and traditionally structured classes (Oliver & Shaver, 1963).

One study will hardly be sufficient to calm the anxiety around the question of what happens to content acquisition when inquiry or problem solving are included in the curriculum. More curricula will have to be tested for effectiveness in transferring content and/or process. In the field of education of the gifted, reports of innovative curricula generally include fascinating descriptions but no substantive data specific to content acquisition. The purpose of the present study was to conduct a comparison of gifted students' content acquisition following traditional or experimental instruction. At the heart of investigation was the need to assess the effectiveness of a curriculum and instructional approach known as *problem-based learning* in an American studies class.

Problem-Based Learning. Problem-based learning was originally developed to introduce the use of meaningful thinking skills in graduate-level medical education (Barrows, 1985). Barrows noted that medical school graduates left their programs with a good foundation of facts but with little skill in the kinds of diagnostic strategies including "hypothetico-deductive" (p. 6) reasoning and reiterative problem solving. Problem-based learning integrates these skills into a content-rich curriculum by making three simultaneous changes in the classroom.

read aloud PBL

The first change is that instruction is initiated by the presentation of an ill-structured problem. Characteristics of the ill-structured problems are that: (a) more information than is initially available is needed to understand the situation/problem and decide what actions are required for resolution; (b) no single formula exists for conducting an investigation to resolve the problem; (c) as new information is obtained, the problem changes; and (d) students can never be 100% sure they have made the "right" decision (Barrows, 1985). Beginning learning with an ill-structured problem also serves as a powerful motivational tool by enticing students with multiple avenues to explore, revealing the romance of the discipline (Whitehead, 1929, p. 17) and stimulating "hot cognition" (Carter 1988, p. 558).

> The emphasis on metacognition represents a vital modernization of the problems-oriented approach.

The second change incorporated into the problem-based classroom is that students are encouraged to take control of the learning process by learning to take responsibility while the teacher reflects on student thinking as a metacognitive coach. In this environment, students become self-assured in their abilities as learners while they simultaneously learn how to select and apply problem-solving strategies that are appropriate to the moment. The emphasis on metacognition represents a vital modernization of the problems-oriented approach. Previous curricula, as advocated by Dewey, Bruner, Gagné, or Piaget, focused directly on thinking skills. However, there is increasing recognition that students need to be judicious monitors of their thinking as well as adept at various reasoning skills (Martorella, 1991; Sternberg, 1988).

A third change is placing students in a carefully selected *stakeholder position*. The stakeholder in a problem-based episode is a person who has some level of authority, accountability, and responsibility for resolving some aspect of the problem. Students are assigned a specific role in each problem they encounter: a forest ranger in a problem about the spotted owl; an archeologist in a problem about finding artifacts at a school construction site; a restaurant association lobbyist in a problem about restrictions on public smoking places. Placing students in specific roles helps to achieve the goals of "situated cognition" and "apprenticeship" associated with problem-based learning. By placing students in the shoes of actual professionals, they learn (a) the way people in different disciplines approach problem solving; (b) the biases, perspectives, and paradigms of interpretation that different professionals bring to the problem-solving process; (c) the subjective element that is always present in real-world problem solving; (d) the necessity of appreciating many approaches to interpreting a problem situation (in the owl example, the economic, environmental, and political approaches); and (e) the complex process of weighing the priorities of different constituents in the problem who have equally compelling, but conflicting, goals.

An important point to be made about problem-based learning is that the problems are carefully structured so students will encounter worthy bodies of knowledge. Students are not just problem solving, they are solving problems that are central to their field(s) of study and are designed around specific educational goals. Thus, content coverage is subsumed within the problem, not eliminated. Margetson (1991) describes the relationship between content and process in problem-based learning:

> Dealing with problems *presupposes* propositional knowledge but does not equate expertise with it, as subject-based views tend to do. Problem-based learning places emphasis on what is needed, on the ability to gain propositional knowledge as required, and to put it to the most valuable use in a given situation. It does not, therefore, deny the importance of "content"—but it does deny that content is best acquired in the abstract, in vast quantities, and memorized in a purely propositional form, to be brought out and "applied" (much) later to problems. Problem-based learning requires a much greater integration of knowing *that* with knowing *how*. (p. 44)

Recently, attempts have been made to translate problem-based learning to the K–12 classroom (Gallagher, Sher, Stepien, & Workman, 1995; Stepien, Gallagher, & Workman, 1993) and to test its effectiveness. Evidence that problem-based learning enhances students' awareness of problem finding as a component of problem solving is promising (Gallagher, Stepien, & Rosenthal, 1992), but it is only one piece of a larger research agenda that faces any new instructional approach.

Study Hypothesis. Because of the assumption that the fact acquisition is sacrificed in "inquiry-oriented" curriculum, a conservative hypothesis was adopted: that students in the problem-based class would acquire significantly less information than students in a traditional instructional setting. Information acquisition was operationally defined as students' recall of factual information on a multiple-choice test without the advantage of specific preparatory study. A multiple-choice test format was selected to test problem-based learning according to the most traditional form of assessment of discrete content acquisition.

METHODS

Subjects

Students in the study attended a three-year, state-supported residential school for students talented in mathematics and science. Students applying to the school completed the SAT in eighth or ninth grade. SAT-Verbal and Mathematics scores in combination with grades; demonstrated interest; and teacher, counselor, and parent recommendations were used as admissions criteria. Admitted students attend the school for their sophomore, junior, and senior high school years.

> The course was designed to teach students key information and concepts . . .

All students who participated in the study were sophomores. There were 93 males and 74 females in the sample. Only students who remained with the same American studies instructor throughout the year-long course were included in the analysis. Students are assigned to their instructor prior to their arrival at the school; therefore, placement of students with instructors is random.

The four American studies instructors in the study all had prior experience teaching American history at the school. All of the instructors held a master's degree in education, history, or social science. Of the four instructors, one taught one section of American studies, two taught two sections each, and one instructor taught three sections. The instructor of the problem-based course taught two sections of American studies. To protect the anonymity of the teachers, code numbers were assigned. The teacher using the problem-based approach was coded as Teacher 3.

Instrument

A multiple-choice test was constructed from a computerized data base of American studies test items created for a well-established American history textbook series (Divine, 1991). Sixty-five items, with a span of items covering American history from European exploration of North America to the Nixon presidential administration, were included on the test. Test construction was consciously designed to replicate a typical end-of-year, multiple-choice, cumulative exam reflective of the American studies course.

Procedure

American Studies

American studies was a year-long, required core course in the sophomore-year curriculum. The course was designed to teach students key information and concepts including: Becoming "Americans," Power and the Framework for Government, the Continuing Revolution: Rights in America, and America's Rise to a World Power. As a course required for graduation, teachers and students alike were aware of the need to succeed in transmitting or learning course content and concepts.

Problem-Based Learning in American Studies

The problem-based class used problems in intermittent post-holes throughout the course. Post-holes represented self-contained learning episodes inserted into the scope and sequence of the course. The length of the post-holes varied, depending on the topic under investigation. Approximately 50% of the school year was devoted to problem-based post-holes. There was no direct instruction of material "covered" during a problem, either before the problems began or after they concluded. To minimize the potential for "traditional" learning while students were engaged in a problem-based episode, no textbook readings were assigned. The textbook was available to students as one of their research resources.

The problems students faced in the problem-based course included dilemmas surrounding Fort Sumter, the Salem witch trials, *Plessy v. Ferguson,* the use of the nuclear bomb on Hiroshima, the development of big business, the formation of the Virginia colonies, the Constitution, Sudbury, and civil rights. The objective of these problems was not to have students discover what really happened in the situation or resolve a question of fact or theory—the usual goal of "inquiry." Rather, the objective was to resolve problems using data and perspectives consistent with the places, people, events, and chronology found in each problem situation.

> Rather, the objective was to resolve problems using data and perspective consistent with the places, people, events, and chronology found in each problem situation.

For example, in one problem about America's rise to world power, students were asked to advise President Truman on a strategy to end the war in the Pacific. The problem they faced was contained in a very brief memo they each received from Secretary of War Stimson that contained the operative sentence: "The President is most anxious to receive your recommendations on how to bring a speedy end to the war, based upon unconditional surrender by the Japanese, and providing for a secure postwar world."

When students arrived for the next class meeting, the first meeting of their "interim committee," they were given a TOP SECRET briefing sheet on the recent detonation of an atomic bomb on the reservation at Los Alamos, New Mexico. Problem solving began with the teacher/tutor asking the committee members to report what information they have about their situation on July 18, 1945 (the date on the top of the memo from the president). By the end of the class period, the students had shared what they already knew about the state of the world and the war in the summer of 1945. More importantly, they identified questions they needed to answer about issues facing the warring parties. Questions generated by the students included: How is the war going in the Pacific? How do American and Japanese casualties compare in the most recent battles? What do we know about the Japanese mentality and the conduct of warfare? How successful has the U.S. blockade and bombing been in slowing the Japanese war effort? How many atomic bombs does the U.S. have? What will it be like to use this weapon in combat? What did the bomb cost? How do the Russians and Americans feel about each other at this point in the war? Will Russia enter the war against Japan? If so, when? What will Russia want in return for participating? Why must we have unconditional surrender?

As the first class meeting closed, these questions were divided among the students and they were directed to the library to find materials that might be helpful for their investigation. With each student responsible for finding information and sharing it as the discussion demanded, the following three or four class sessions were devoted to developing a comprehensive understanding of the situation in the Pacific. As the collaborative data gathering, sharing, and analysis developed, the teacher/tutor continually asked students to describe the shifting "problem" of ending the war. Carefully, the tutor began to coach the class as they built strategy options that seemed feasible. Finally, based upon a request from the president that recommendations be forwarded immediately, the class/committee turned its complete attention to strategy formation. Various options were developed in detail. In light of the three criteria identified in the president's original request, critiques of each option were prepared. With all of the options spelled out, the class then had to grapple with the task of choosing which of the inherently limited options they would recommend. After making their recommendation, the students' decisions were compared with the actual historical account; similarities and differences in decisions were discussed as a part of debriefing the problem.

Instruction in Comparison Classrooms
Instruction varied from classroom to classroom; however, the comparison classrooms were different from the problem-based classroom in several respects. First, although higher order thinking (synthesis, evaluation) was a part of each course, the comparison classes were dominated by teacher presentation of information. Second, a standard textbook was used as a basis for instruction in comparison classes. Any classroom discussion or higher order thinking activity either introduced or reinforced reading in the texts. Third, neither inquiry nor problem solving was systematically or routinely used as a part of instruction in any of the comparison classrooms.

Instead, the classes were marked by intermittent use of inquiry and higher order thinking activities. Little or no problem-solving activities were integrated into instruction in the comparison classes.

Pre- and Posttesting

Multiple-choice test scores of students in either traditional or problem-based classrooms were compared at the beginning and of end of the school year to determine the effect of the problem-based approach on a standard measure of achievement. The intent of the study was to measure the growth in knowledge that students stored in stable memory. Short-term knowledge acquisition resulting from last-minute study for a test would interfere with the measurement of more meaningful knowledge acquisition. In order to maximize the potential to measure stable knowledge acquisition, students were not informed of the test ahead of time. To counter against any resulting test anxiety, students were also informed that test results would not be used in the calculation of their course grades. As an added precaution, instructors were not allowed to see the test to avoid a teaching-to-the-test effect, especially in the problem-based classroom.

> . . . instructors were not allowed to see the test to avoid a teaching-to-the-test effect . . .

The pretest was administered in each of the six sections of American studies shortly after the beginning of the school year. The posttest was administered in March of the school year well before study for exams would begin. After the posttest was administered, the instructor of the problem-based course was asked to mark the questions that students were exposed to directly in the problem-based portions of the course as opposed to items that they might have learned through direct instruction. Thirty-one of the thirty-two items the instructor identified as instructional targets were introduced during a problem post-hole.

Data Analysis

Initial analyses were conducted using student entrance scores on the SAT Mathematics subtest, the SAT Verbal subtest, the Test of Standard Written English, as well as the qualitative performance and overall ratings from the student's application to the school. These analyses established that ability levels were not significantly different across classrooms, eliminating the potential for bias in distribution of students across classes.

A one-way analysis of variance (ANOVA) was conducted on pretest data to test for possible differences in ability and/or experience among instructors. A change score (posttest-pretest) was calculated and used to compute the mean gain in each class. A second one-way ANOVA was conducted on the gain scores to test the study hypothesis. Although analysis of covariance (ANCOVA) is generally preferable for this kind of data, covarying out pretest scores to adjust for initial ability, the equivalent mean gain score was conducted in this case. The decision to use the mean gain score test was based on the goal of the research, which was to help the instructors in the study learn more about their practice. The analysis technique selected had to meet the dual criteria of being both appropriate and accessible to teachers unschooled in statistics. The mean gains score test achieves similar results as the more abstract ANCOVA and still allows for easy transfer from the statistical test to familiar measures of student achievement. All data analyses were conducted using the SPSS-PC+ statistical package (Norusis, 1991).

RESULTS

Analysis of Sample Characteristics

A one-way ANOVA of entrance scores of students enrolled with each teacher revealed no significant differences in academic aptitude as measured by the SAT Mathematics and Verbal subtests and the Test of Standard Written English. Analysis of the performance rating and the overall rating from the school application also showed no significant difference, indicating that students were equally distributed among instructors on traits including academic motivation and prior academic experiences. Means and standard deviations on these measures are presented in Table 1.

The one-way ANOVA testing for significant differences among the classes on the pretest was also nonsignificant, establishing that students had acquired and retained similar amounts of information in American history prior to their sophomore year in high school. Results of this ANOVA are presented in Table 2a.

Table 1
Average Scores on Entrance Scores by Instructor
(sd in parentheses)

	Teacher 1 (n = 43)	Teacher 2 (n = 59)	Teacher 3 (n = 37)	Teacher 4 (n = 21)
SAT-M`	622.09 (94.04)	641.19 (85.24)	625.68 (57.86)	643.33 (91.01)
SAT-V	524.88 (89.53)	525.93 (71.92)	520.81 (53.97)	512.38 (85.08)
TSWE	52.49 (6.65)	53.59 (5.21)	52.41 (5.37)	51.10 (6.16)
PERF	67.21 (7.58)	66.86 (7.36)	66.89 (7.49)	67.38 (6.05)
OA	67.21 (6.84)	67.46 (7.27)	67.70 (7.23)	69.05 (4.90)

Table 2a
Analysis of Variance of Pretest Scores by Instructor

Source of Variance	Sum of Squares	df	Mean Square	F	Sign. of F
Main Effect: Teacher	38.956	3	12.985	.395	.757
Explained	38.956	3	12.985	.395	.757
Residual	5363.858	163	32.907		
Total	5402.814	166	32.547		

Hypothesis Testing

An ANOVA was conducted using mean gain scores as the dependent variable after establishing a relatively equal background in knowledge through the ANOVA of pretest scores. The analysis of gain score by instructor resulted in significant differences between teach-

Table 2b
Analysis of Variance of Mean Gain Scores by Instructor

Source of Variance	Sum of Squares	df	Mean Square	F	Sign. of F
Between Groups	811.51	3	270.503	11.888	.000
Within Groups	3708.912	163	22.750		
Total	4520.419	166	32.547		

ers $F(3, 163) = 11.89$, $p < .000$. A multiple comparisons analysis using the Tukey b test revealed that even though the problem-based learning teacher, Teacher 3, had the highest gain, the gain was only statistically significantly different from Teacher 2. Teachers 1 and 4 were also significantly higher than Teacher 2, but no significant difference was observed among Teachers 1, 3, and 4. A complete report of the results of the ANOVA is presented in Table 2b. Pretest and posttest scores for each instructor are presented in Table 3.

Table 3
Average Pretest and Posttest Scores by Instructor
(sd in Parentheses)

	Pretest	Posttest	Gain Score
Teacher 1 (n = 47)	27.96 (6.20)	31.21 (6.49)	3.26**
Teacher 2 (n = 62)	27.85 (5.81)	26.76 (6.89)	−1.10
Teacher 3* (n = 37)	26.73 (4.98)	30.51 (5.81)	3.78**
Teacher 4 (n = 21)	27.38 (5.66)	30.67 (6.39)	3.29**

* Teacher 3 was the problem-based learning instructor
**significantly higher than Teacher 2, p<.05

DISCUSSION

Based on the finding of no significant differences between Teacher 3, who taught the problem-based course, and Teachers 1 and 4, the hypothesis that problem-based learning would result in lower levels of fact acquisition was rejected. To become standard classroom practice, inquiry-based approaches must be shown to "do no harm" in terms of content acquisition. The results of this study provide assurance of just that. Students in the problem-based course retained as much factual information as students in other classes. Indeed, they had the highest average gain of any group. These findings add to the growing body of evidence supporting the claim that teaching for depth of understanding also facilitates retention of facts. In combination with other research literature demonstrating that instruction for higher order thinking skills also promotes the development of important "value-added" skills and dispositions, the argument in favor of using approaches like problem-based learning gains additional strength.

> Students in the problem-based course retained as much factual information as students in other classes.

Other findings of the study are worthy of some note. Especially interesting was the small increase in gain scores on the 65-item multiple-choice test, which may seem to challenge the meaningfulness of the analysis. However, small gains are generally typical of testing situations that hold "low stakes" for students. Analysis of studies such as the NAEP reveal that when testing occurs without opportunity for last-minute study or the "high-stakes" consequence of a grade, average knowledge gain tends to be around one-third of a standard deviation (Mullis, Dossey, Foertsch, Jones, & Gentile, 1991). Regardless of the instructional approach, students in this study failed to gain more than an average of 3–4 points over the course of the year. Despite the fact that a gain of 3–4 points is substantially higher than one-third of the standard deviation in any given class, this finding raises the question of how much information students really retain over time. Traditionally, school tests—and, increasingly, standardized achievement tests—are preceded with some form of drilling or studying, increasing the store of information in short-term memory. The average-gain scores observed in the current study suggest that very little of the short-term gain is sustained and that what is often referred to in the literature as fact acquisition may be little more than a temporary stuffing that is removed as soon as the need disappears. Additional research using testing for long-term acquisition could add valuable information to the depth-versus-breadth debate, especially if the results here were replicated.

Doubtless the results achieved here rest on *combining* process-based instruction with meaningful content. Skills-based critical-thinking programs that do not have the same emphasis on using skills in the context of a body of knowledge important to a discipline or across disciplines may not achieve similar results. The current findings can only be generalized to critical-thinking programs that are founded on a philosophy of integrating process and content.

An important qualification to be made about the present findings is that it is subject to all of the limitations common to action- or classroom-based research, which is restricted by the unique characteristics of school, staff, and students. With only one teacher using the problem-based approach, it is impossible to determine whether the effect was due solely to the quality of the curricular approach, the potential influence of the Hawthorne effect must also be considered. Finally, while results are promising for gifted students, they cannot automatically be generalized beyond the population; replication with samples of students with different levels of ability are also necessary to test content-based effectiveness of this technique in the general student population. While all of these restrictions may constrain the interpretations of our findings, they are balanced by the value of action-based investigation, which lies in the integration of research into the real complexities and limitations of the classroom and provides an added authenticity that more carefully controlled laboratory studies lack.

This research represents a single step in what is a much larger research agenda to investigate the effectiveness of problem-based learning. Additional studies should build on these findings, including research using other instructors, different kinds of students, and different subject areas. Research into the effect of problem-based learning on student cognition and affect would provide a valuable litmus test to the approach. Other research designed to test the value of similarly innovative approaches could replicate current findings and broaden the available literature on instructional approaches.

Questions of the difference between testing for long-term versus short-term acquisition of information are also raised in the current data. Even with an extensive research agenda still to be fulfilled, we take these findings as promising support of problem-based learning as one of the techniques providing students with a meaningful exposure to the content and the practices of a discipline.

Acknowledgements: We would like to gratefully thank the social science team at the Illinois Mathematics and Science Academy for their assistance in this project. This study was funded in part with a grant from the Hitachi Foundation.

REFERENCES

Barrows, H. (1985). *How to design a problem-based learning curriculum in the pre-clinical years.* New York: Springer-Verlag.

Bradley Commission on History in the Schools (1989). Building a history curriculum: Guidelines for teaching history in schools. In P. Gagnon (Ed.), *Historical literacy* (pp. 16–42). New York: Macmillan.

Brown, R. (1991). *Schools of thought: How the politics of literacy shape thinking in the classroom.* San Francisco: Jossey-Bass.

Carter, M. (1988). Problem solving reconsidered: A pluralistic theory of problems. *College English, 50,* 551-565.

Chand, I., & Runco, M. A. (1993). Problem finding skills as components in the creative process. *Personality and Individual Differences, 14*(1), 155–162.

Committee for Economic Development (1985). *Investing in our children.* Washington, DC: Author.

Divine, R. A. (1991). *America, past and present.* New York: Harper Collins.

Ehman, L. H. (1969). An analysis of the relationships of selected educational variables with the political socialization of high school students. *American Educational Research Journal, 6,* 559–580.

Evans, R. W. (1989). A dream unrealized: A brief look at the history of issue-centered approaches. *The Social Studies, 80,* 178–184.

Gagnon, P. (Ed.). (1989). *Historical literacy.* New York: Macmillan.

Gallagher, S. A. (1994). Middle school predictors of science persistence. *Journal for Research in Science Teaching, 31,* 721–734.

Gallagher, S. A., Sher, B. T., Stepien, W. J., & Workman, D. (1995). Implementing problem-based learning in the science classroom. *School Science and Mathematics, 126*–146.

Gallagher, S. A., Stepien, W. J., & Rosenthal, H. (1992). Changes in talented students' spontaneously elicited problem solving steps as a result of problem-based instruction. *Gifted Child Quarterly, 36,* 195–201.

Girault, E. S. (1971). Current trends in problem solving. In R. E. Gross & R. H. Muessig (Eds.), *Problem-centered social studies instruction: Approaches to reflective teaching* (pp. 70–82). Washington, DC: National Council for the Social Studies.

Gross, R. E. (1989). Reasons for the limited acceptance of the problems approach. *The Social Studies, 80,* 185–186.

Hunt, M. P., & Metcalf, L. E. (1971). Problems approach—theory. In R. E. Gross & R. H. Muessig (Eds.), *Problem-centered social studies instruction: Approaches to reflective teaching* (pp. 1–11). Washington, DC: National Council for the Social Studies.

Knight, S. L., & Waxman, H. C. (1991). Students' cognition and classroom instruction. In H. C. Waxman & H. J. Walberg (Eds.), *Effective teaching: Current research.* Berkeley, CA: McCutchan.

Maker, C. J. (1982). *Curriculum development for the gifted.* Rockville, MD: Aspen.

Margetson, D. (1991). Why is problem-based learning a challenge? In D. Boud & G. Feletti (Eds.), *The challenge of problem-based learning.* New York: St. Martin's.

Martorella, P. (1991). Knowledge and concept development in social studies. In J. P. Shaver (Ed.), *Handbook of research on social studies teaching and learning* (pp. 370–384). New York: Macmillan.

Mullis, I. V. S., & Jenkins, L. B. (1988). *The science report card: Elements of risk and recovery.* Princeton, NJ: Educational Testing Service.

Mullis, I. V., Dossey, J. A., Foertsch, M. A., Jones, L. R., & Gentile, C. A. (1991). *Trends in academic programs: Achievement of U.S. students in science, 1969–1990: Mathematics, 1973–1990; Reading, 1971–1990; and Writing, 1984–1990.* Washington, DC: U.S. Department of Education.

National Education Association (1916). *The social studies in secondary education. A report of the Committee on Social Studies on the Reorganization of Secondary Education* (Bulletin #28). Washington, DC: U.S. Department of the Interior, Bureau of Education.

Newell, A. (1980). Reasoning, problem solving, and decision processes: The problem as a fundamental category. In. R. S. Nickerson (Ed.), *Attention and*

Performance VIII: Proceedings of the Eighth International Symposium on Attention and Performance (pp. 693–718). Hillsdale, NJ: Lawrence Erlbaum.

Newmann, F. M. (1990). Higher order thinking in teaching social studies: A rational for the assessment of classroom thoughtfulness. *Journal of Curriculum Studies, 22*(1), 41–56.

Norusis, M. J. (1991). *The SPSS guide to data analysis.* Chicago, IL: SPSS.

Okuda, S. M., Runco, M. A., & Berger, D. E. (1991). Creativity and the finding and solving of real-world problems. *Journal of Psychoeducational Assessment, 9,* 45–53.

Oliver, D. W., & Shaver, J. P. (1963). *The analysis of public controversy: A study of citizenship education. A report to the U.S. Office of Education.* Cambridge, MA: Harvard Graduate School of Education, The Laboratory for Research in Instruction.

Onosko, J. J. (1991). Barriers to the promotion of higher order thinking in social studies. *Theory and Research in Social Education, 19,* 341–366.

Parker, W. C. (1991). Achieving thinking and decision-making objectives in social studies. In J. P. Shaver (Ed.), *Handbook of research on social studies teaching and learning* (pp. 345–356). New York: Macmillan.

Patrick, J. J. (1991). *Achievement of knowledge by high school students in core subjects of the social studies.* Bloomington: Indiana University. (ERIC Document Reproduction Service No. EDO-SO-91–1).

Rutherford, F. J., & Ahlgren, A. (1990). *Science for all Americans.* NY: Basic Books.

Spiro, R. J., Vispoel, W., Schmitz, J., Samarapugavan, A., & Boerger, A. (1987). Knowledge acquisitions for application: Cognitive flexibility and transfer in complex content domains. In B. C. Britton (Ed.), *Executive control processes (pp. 177–199).* Hillsdale, NJ: Lawrence Erlbaum.

Spiro, R. J., Feltovich, P. J., Coulson, R. L., & Anderson, D. K. (1989). Multiple analogies for complex concepts: Antidotes for analogy-induced misconception in advanced knowledge acquisition. In S. Voaniadov & A. Ortony (Eds.), *Similarity and analogical reasoning.* New York: Cambridge University Press.

Stepien, W. J., & Gallagher, S. A. (1993). Problem-based learning: As authentic as it gets. *Educational Leadership, 50*(7), 25–29.

Stepien, W. J., Gallagher, S. A., & Workman, D. (1993). Problem-based learning for traditional and interdisciplinary classrooms. *Journal for the Education of the Gifted, 16,* 338–357.

Sternberg, R. J. (1988). *The triarchic mind: A new theory of intelligence.* New York: Viking.

Taba, H. (1962). *Curriculum development, theory, and practice.* New York: Harcourt, Brace, & World.

Torney-Purta, J. (1986). Predictors of global awareness and concern among secondary school students. Columbus: Ohio State University, The Mercer Center. (ERIC Document Reproduction Service No. ED 271 364)

VanSicle, R. L., & Hoge, J. D. (1991). Higher cognitive thinking skills in social studies: Concepts and critiques. *Theory and Research in Social Education, 19,* 152–172.

Voss, J. F. (1989). Problem solving and the educational process. In A. Lesgold & R. Glaser (Eds.), *Foundations for a psychology of education* (pp. 351–394). Hillsdale, NJ: Lawrence Erlbaum.

Whitehead, A. N. (1967). *The aims of education and other essays* (2nd ed.). New York: Free Press.

Wiggins, G. (1989). The futility of trying to teach everything of importance. *Educational Leadership, 47*(3), 44–59.

Problem Based Learning: An Instructional Model and Its Constructivist Framework

by John R. Savery and Thomas M. Duffy

It is said that there's nothing so practical as good theory. It may also be said that there's nothing so theoretically interesting as good practice.[1] This is particularly true of efforts to relate constructivism as a theory of learning to the practice of instruction. Our goal in this article is to provide a clear link between the theoretical principles of constructivism, the practice of instructional design, and the practice of teaching. We will begin with a basic characterization of constructivism, identifying what we believe to be the central principles in learning and understanding. We will then identify and elaborate on eight instructional principles for the design of a constructivist learning environment. Finally, we will examine what we consider to be one of the best exemplars of a contructivist learning environment—Problem Based Learning, as described by Barrows (1985, 1986, 1992).

CONSTRUCTIVISM

Constructivism is a philosophical view on how we come to understand or know. It is, in our mind, most closely attuned to the pragmatic philosophy of Richard Rorty (1991). Space limitations for this article prevent an extensive discussion of this philosophical base, but we would commend to the interested reader the work of Rorty (1991) as well as vonGlasersfeld (1989). We will characterize the philosophical view in terms of these primary propositions:

1. *Understanding is in our interactions with the environment.* This is the core concept of constructivism. We cannot talk about what is learned separately from how it is learned, as if a variety of experiences all lead to the same understanding. Rather, what we understand is a function of the content, the context, the activity of

the learner, and, perhaps most importantly, the goals of the learner. Since understanding is an individual construction, we cannot share understandings, but rather, we can test the degree to which our individual understandings are compatible. An implication of this proposition is that cognition is not just within the individual, but rather it is part of the entire context, i.e., cognition is distributed.

2. *Cognitive conflict or puzzlement is the stimulus for learning and determines the organization and nature of what is learned.* When we are in a learning environment, there is some stimulus or goal for learning—the learner has a purpose for being there. That goal is not only the stimulus for learning, but it is a primary factor in determining what the learner attends to, what prior experience the learner brings to bear in constructing an understanding, and, basically, what understanding is eventually constructed. In Dewey's terms, it is the "problematic" that leads to and is the organizer for learning (Dewey, 1938; Roschelle, 1992). For Piaget it is the need for accommodation when current experience cannot be assimilated in existing schema (Piaget, 1977; vonGlasersfeld, 1989). We prefer to talk about the learner's "puzzlement" as being the stimulus and organizer for learning, since this more readily suggest both intellectual and pragmatic goals for learning. The important point, however, is that it is the goal of the learner that is central in considering what is learned.

3. *Knowledge evolves through social negotiation and through the evaluation of the viability of individual understandings.* The social environment is critical to the development of our individual understanding as well as to the development of the body or proposition we call knowledge. At the first, or individual level, other individuals are primary mechanism for testing our understanding. Collaborative groups are important because we can test our own understanding and examine the understanding of others as a mechanism for enriching, interweaving, and expanding our understanding of particular issues or phenomena. As vonGlasersfeld (1989) has noted, other people are the greatest source of alternative views to challenge our current views and hence to serve as the source of puzzlement that stimulates new learning. The second role of the social environment is to develop a set of propositions we call knowledge. We seek propositions that are compatible with our individual constructions or understanding of the world. Thus, facts are facts because there is widespread agreement, not because there is some ultimate truth to the fact. It was once a fact that the earth was flat and the sun

revolved around the earth. More recently, it was fact that the smallest particles of matter were electrons, protons, and neurons. These were facts because there was general agreement that the concepts and principles arising from these views provided the best interpretation of our world. The same search for viability holds in our daily life. In both cases, concepts that we call knowledge do not represent some ultimate truth, but are simply the most viable interpretation of our experiential world (see Resnick, 1987). The important consideration in this third proposition is that all views, or all constructions, are not equally viable. Constructivism is not a desconstructivist view in which all constructions are equal simply because they are personal experiences. Rather, we seek viability, and thus we must test understandings to determine how adequately they allow us to interpret and function in our world. Our social environment is primary in providing alternative views and additional information against which we can test the viability of our understanding and in building the set of propositions (knowledge) compatible with those understandings (Cunningham, Duffy, & Knuth, 1991). Hence we discuss social negotiation of meaning and understanding based on viability.

> Concepts that we call knowledge do not represent some ultimate truth, but are simply the most viable interpretation of our experiential world.

INSTRUCTIONAL PRINCIPLES

The constructivist propositions outlined above suggest a set of instructional principles that can guide the practice of teaching and the design of learning environments. All too often when we discuss principles of teaching we hear the retort, "But we already do that. . ." While that assertion may well be accurate, too often the claim is based on the principle in isolation rather than in the context of the overall framework. Indeed, everyone "does" collaborative groups; the real issue is what the goal is in using collaborative groups, since that determines the details of how they are used and how they are contextualized in the overall instructional framework.

We think Lebow (1993) has hit upon a strategy for summarizing the constructivist framework in a way that may help with the interpretation of the instructional strategies. He talks about the shift in values when one takes a constructivist perspective. He notes that:

> . . . traditional educational technology values of replicability, reliability, communication, and control (Heinich, 1984) contrast sharply with the seven primary constructivist values of collaboration, personal autonomy, generativity, reflectivity, active engagement, personal relevance, and pluralism. (1993, p.5)

We agree with Lebow and would propose that this value system serve to guide the reader's interpretation of our instructional principles as well as the interpretation of the problem based learning environment we will describe. The instructional principles deriving from constructivism are as follows:

1. *Anchor all learning activities to a larger task or problem.* That is, learning must have a purpose beyond, "It is assigned." We learn in order to be able to function more effectively in our world. The purpose of any learning activity should be clear to the learner. Individual learning activities can be of any type—the important issue is that the learner clearly perceives and accepts the relevance of the specific learning activities in relation to the larger task complex (Cognition & Technology Group at Vanderbilt, 1992; Honebein, Duffy, & Fishman, 1993).

2. *Support the learner in developing ownership for the overall problem or task.* Instructional programs typically specify learning objectives and perhaps even engage the learner in a project, assuming that the leaner will understand and buy into the relevance and value of the problem (Blumenfeld, Soloway, Marx, Krajcik, Guzdial, & Palincsar, 1991). Unfortunately, it is too often the case that the learners do not accept the goal of the instructional program, but rather simply focus on passing the test or putting in their time. No matter what we specify as the learning objective, the goals of the learner will largely determine what is learned. Hence, it is essential that the goals the learner brings to the environment are consistent with our instructional goals.

There are two ways of doing this. First, we may solicit problems from the learners and use those as the stimulus for learning activities. This is basically what happens in graduate schools when qualifying exams require the student to prepare publishable papers in each of several domains (Honebein *et al.*, 1993). Scardamalia and Bereiter (1991) have shown that even elementary students can initiate questions (puzzlements) that can serve as the foundation of learning activities in traditional school subject matter. In essence, the strategy is to define a territory and then to work with the learner in developing meaningful problems or tasks in the domain. Alternatively, we can establish a problem in such a way that the learners will readily adopt the problem as their own. We see this strategy in the design of the Jasper series for teaching mathematics (Cognition & Technology Group at Vanderbilt, 1992) and in many simulation environments.[2] In either case, it is important to engage the learner in meaningful dialogue to help bring the problem or task home to that learner.

> ... the goals of the learner will largely determine what is learned.

3. *Design an authentic task.* An authentic learning environment does *not* mean that the fourth grader should be placed in an authentic physics lab, nor that he or she should grapple with the same problems with which adult physicists deal. Rather, the learner should engage in scientific activities which present the same "type" of cognitive challenges. An authentic learning environment is one in which the cognitive demands, i.e., the thinking required, are consistent with the cognitive demands in the environment for which we are preparing the leaner (Honebein et al., 1993). Thus, we do not want the learner to learn about history but rather to engage in the construction or use of history in ways that a historian or a good citizen would. Similarly, we do not want the leaner to study science— memorizing a text on science or executing scientific procedures as dictated—but rather to engage in scientific discourse and problem solving (see Bereiter, 1994; Duffy, in press, Honebein *et al.*, 1993). Allowing the problem to be generated by the learner, an option discussed above, does not automatically assure authenticity. It may well require discussion and negotiation with the learner to develop a problem or task which is authentic in its cognitive demands and for which the learner can take ownership.

4. *Design the task and the learning environment to reflect the complexity of the environment they should be able to function in at the end of learning.* Rather than simplifying the environment for the learner, we seek to support the learner working in the complex environment. This is consistent with both cognitive apprenticeship (Collins, Brown, & Newman, 1989) and cognitive flexibility theory (Spiro *et al.*, 1992) and reflects the importance of context in determining the understanding we have of any particular concept or principle.

5. *Give the learner ownership of the process used to develop a solution.* Learners must have ownership of the learning or problem-solving process as well as ownership of the problem itself. Frequently, teachers will give students ownership of the problem, but dictate the process for working on that problem. Thus, they may dictate that a particular problem solving or critical thinking methodology be used or that particular content domains be "learned." For example, in some problem based learning frameworks, the problem is presented along with the learning objectives and the assigned readings related to the problem. Thus, the student is told what to study and what to learn in relation to the problem. Clearly, with this pre-specification of activities, the students are not going to be engaged in authentic thinking and problem solving in that domain. Rather than being a stimulus for problem solving and self-directed learning, the problem serves merely as an example. The teacher's role should be to challenge the learner's thinking—not to dictate or attempt to proceduralize that thinking.

> **Design the learning environment to support and challenge the learners' thinking.**

6. *Design the learning environment to support and challenge the learners' thinking.* While we advocate giving the learner ownership of the problem and the solution process, it is not the case that *any* activity or *any* solution is adequate. Indeed, the critical goal is to support the learner in becoming an effective worker/thinker in the particular domain. The teacher must assume the roles of consultant and coach. The most critical teaching activity is in the questions the teacher asks the learner in that consulting and coaching activity. It is essential that the teacher *value as well as challenge* the learner's thinking. The teacher must not take over thinking for the learner by telling the learner what to do or how to think, but rather teaching should be done by inquiring at the "leading edge" of the learner's thinking (Fosnot, 1989). This is different from the widely used Socratic method wherein the teacher has the "right" answer and it is the student's task to guess/deduce through logical questioning that correct answer. The concept of a learning scaffold and the zone of proximal development, as described by Vygotsky (1978), is a more accurate representation of the learning exchange/interaction between the teacher and the student.

Learners use information resources (all media types) and instructional materials (all media types) as sources of information. The materials do not teach, but rather support the learners' inquiry or performance. This does not negate any kind of instructional resource—it only specifies the reason for using the resource. Thus, if domain specific problem solving is the skill to be learned, then a simulation which confronts the learner with problem situations within that domain might be appropriate. If proficient typing is required for some larger context, certainly a drill and practice program is one option that might be present.

7. *Encourage testing ideas against alternative views and alternative contexts.* Knowledge is socially negotiated. The quality or depth of one's understanding can only be determined in a social environment where we can see if our understanding can accommodate the issues and views of others and to see if there are points of view which we could usefully incorporate into our understanding. The importance of a learning community where ideas are discussed and understanding enriched is critical to the design of an effective learning environment. The use of collaborative learning groups as a part of the overall leaning environment we have described provides one strategy for achieving this learning community (CTGV, 1994; Cunningham, Duffy, & Knuth, 1991; Scardamalia *et al.*, 1992). Other projects support collaboration by linking learners over electronic communication networks as they work on a common task; e.g., CoVis (Edelson & O'Neil, 1994), LabNet (Ruopp *et al.*, 1993), provide an alternative framework.

8. *Provide opportunity for and support reflection on both the content learned and the process.* An important goal of instruction is to develop skills of self-regulation—to become independent. Teachers should model reflective thinking throughout the learning process and support the learners in reflecting on the strategies for learning as well as what was learned (Clift, Houston & Pugach, 1990; Schön, 1987).

In the next section we will explore how these eight instructional principles are realized in the problem-based learning approach.

PROBLEM BASED LEARNING

The instructional design principles, implemented within the framework of the values outlined by Lebow (1993), can lead to a wide variety of learning environments. A number of environments reflecting these principles are described in Duffy and Jonassen (1992) and Duffy, Lowyck, and Jonassen (1993). Further, the elaboration and application of these principles to specific contexts is described in Brooks and Brooks (1993), Duffy (in press), and Fosnot (1989). In our own examination of learning environments, however, we have found one application that seems to us to almost ideally capture the principles—the problem based learning model of Howard Barrows (1985, 1992).

Problem Based Learning (PBL), as a general model, was developed in medical education in the mid-1950's, and since that time it has been refined and implemented in over sixty medical schools. The most widespread application of the PBL approach has been in the first two years of medical science curricula, where it replaces the traditional lecture based approach to anatomy, pharmacology, physiology, etc. The model has been adopted in an increasing number of other areas, including business schools (Milter & Stinson, 1994), schools of education (Bridges & Hallinger, 1992; Duffy, 1994); architecture, law, engineering, social work (Boud & Feletti, 1991); and high school (Barrows & Myers, 1993).

> As with any instructional model, there are many strategies for implementing PBL.

As with any instructional model, there are many strategies for implementing PBL. Rather than attempting to provide a general characterization of PBL, we would like to focus on Barrows' model (Barrows, 1992) to provide a concrete sense of the implementation of this process in medical school. First we will present a general scenario, using the medical environment as the focus, and then examine some of the key elements in some detail.

When students enter medical school, typically they are divided into groups of five, and each group is assigned a facilitator. The students are then presented a problem in the form of a patient entering with presenting symptoms. The students' task is to diagnose the patient and to provide a rationale for that diagnosis and a recommended treatment. The process for working on the problem is outlined in Figure 1. The following paragraphs cover the highlights of that process.

Figure 1
The Problem Based Learning Process

STARTING A NEW CLASS

1. Introductions
2. Climate Setting (including teacher/tutor role)

STARTING A NEW PROBLEM

1. Set the problem.
2. Bring the problem home (students internalize problem)
3. Describe the product/performance required
4. Assign tasks (Scribe 1 at the board, Scribe 2 copying from the board, and reference person)

IDEAS (Hypotheses)	FACTS	LEARNING ISSUES	ACTION PLAN
Students' conjectures regarding the problem—may involve problem causation, effect, possible resolutions, etc.	A growing synthesis of information obtained through inquiry, important to the hypotheses generated	Students' list of what they need to know or understand in order to complete the problem task	Things that need to be done in order to complete the task

5. Reasoning through the problem
   What you do with the columns on the board

IDEAS (Hypotheses)	FACTS	LEARNING ISSUES	ACTION PLAN
Expand/focus	Synthesize & re-synthesize	Identify/justify	Formulate plan

6. Commitment as to probable outcome (although much may need to be learned)
7. Learning issue shaping/assignment
8. Resource identification
9. Schedule follow-up

Figure 1 continued on next page

Figure 1 cont.

PROBLEM FOLLOW-UP

1. Resources used and their critique
2. Reassess the problem
    What you do with the columns on the board

IDEAS (Hypotheses)	FACTS	LEARNING ISSUES	ACTION PLAN
Revise	Apply new knowledge and re-synthesize	Identify new (if necessary)	Redesign decisions

PERFORMANCE PRESENTATION

AFTER CONCLUSION OF PROBLEM

1. Knowledge abstraction and summary (develop definitions, diagrams, lists, concepts, abstractions, principles)
2. Self-evaluation (followed by comments from the group)
    • reasoning through the problem
    • digging out information using good resources
    • assisting the group with its tasks
    • gaining or refining knowledge

Taken from Barrows and Myers (1993).

The students begin the problem "cold"—they do not know what the problem will be until it is presented. They discuss the problem, generating hypotheses based on whatever experience or knowledge they have, identifying relevant facts in the case, and identifying learning issues. The learning issues are topics of any sort deemed of potential relevance to this problem and which the group of members feel they do not understand as well as they should. A session is not complete until each student had an opportunity to verbally reflect on his or her current beliefs about the diagnosis (i.e., commit to a temporary position), and assume responsibility for particular learning issues that were identified. Note that there are no pre-specified objectives presented to the students. The students generate the learning issues (objectives) based on their analysis of the problem.

After the session, the students all engage in self-directed learning. There are no assigned texts. Rather, the students are totally responsible for gathering the information from the available medical library and computer database resources. Additionally, particular faculty are designated to be available as consultants (as they would be for any physician in the real world). The students may go to the consultants, seeking information.

After self-directed learning, the students meet again. They begin by evaluating resources—what was most useful and what was not so useful. They then begin working on the problem with this new level of understanding. Note that they do not simply tell what they learned. Rather, they use that learning in re-examining the problem. This cycle may repeat itself if new learning issues arise— problems in the medical school program last anywhere from a week to three weeks.

Assessment at the end of the process is in terms of peer- and self-evaluation.

Milter and Stinson (1994) use a similar approach in an MBA program at Ohio University, and there the problems last between five and eight weeks (see also Stinson, 1994). In our own implementation, we are using one problem that lasts the entire semester. Of course, in the MBA program and in our own, the problems have multiple sub-problems that engage the students.

Assessment at the end of the process is in terms of peer- and self-evaluation. There are no tests in the medical school curriculum. The assessment includes evaluation (with suggestions for improvement) in three areas: self-directed learning, problem solving, and skills as a group member. While the students must pass the Medical Board exam after two years, this is outside of the curriculum structure.[3] However, tests as part of the PBL curriculum are not precluded. For example, one high school teacher we know who uses the PBL approach designs traditional tests based on what the students have identified as learning issues. Thus, rather than a pre-specification of what is to be learned, the assessment focuses on the issues the learners have identified.

That is an overview of the process in the medical school. Now we will comment on a few of the critical features.

Learning Goals

The design of this environment is meant to simulate, and hence engage the learner in, the problem solving behavior that it is hoped a practicing physician would be engaged in. Nothing is simplified or pre-specified for the learner. The facilitator assumes a major role in modeling the metacognitive thinking associated with the problem solving process. Hence this is a cognitive apprenticeship environment with scaffolding designed to support the learner in developing the metacognitive skills.

Within the context of this cognitive apprenticeship environment, there are goals related to self-directed learning, content knowledge, and problem solving. To be successful, students must develop the self-directed learning skills needed in the medical field. They must be able to develop strategies for identifying learning issues and locating, evaluating, and learning from resources relevant to that issue. The entire problem solving process is designed to aid the students in developing the hypothetico-deductive problem solving model which centers around hypothesis generation and evaluation. Finally, there are specific content learning objectives associated with each problem. Since the students have responsibility for the problem, there is no guarantee that all of the content area objectives will be realized in a given problem. However, any given content objective occurs in several problems, and hence if it does not arise in one, it will almost certainly arise in one of the other problems.

Problem Generation

There are two guiding forces in developing problems. First, the problems must raise the concepts and principles relevant to the content domain. Thus, the process begins with first identifying the primary concepts or principles that a student must learn. Milter and Stinson working in the MBA program and Barrows working with medical education polled the faculty to identify the most important concepts or principles in their area. This, of course, generates considerable debate and discussion—it is not a matter of a simple survey. In developing high school PBL curricula, Myers and Barrows (personal communication) used the learning objectives identified by the state for grade and content domains.

Second, the problems must be "real." In the medical school, the patients are real patients. Indeed, Barrows worked with the presenting physician in gathering the details on the case. Milter and Stinson in the MBA program use problems such as "Should AT&T buy NCR?" These problems change each year so as to address current business issues. At the high school level, Myers and Barrows have developed problems such as:

- Do asteroids in space pose a problem, and if so, what should we be doing about it?
- What caused the flooding in the Midwest in 1993 and what should be done to prevent it in the future?

We are still developing problems and sub-problems for our Corporate and Community Education program. One of the problems currently being developed relates to the numerous PCB sites around Bloomington, Indiana, and the general public apathy about cleaning up these sites. The problem is basically:

- What do citizens need to know about the PCB problem and how should that information be presented to encourage them to be active citizens in the discussion?

There are three reasons why the problems must address real issues. First, because the students are open to explore all dimension of the problem, there is a real difficulty in creating a rich problem with a consistent set of information. Second, real problems tend to engage learners more—there is a larger context of familiarity with the problem. Finally, students want to know the outcome of the problem— what is being done about the flood, did AT&T buy NCR, what was the problem with the patient? These outcomes are not possible with artificial problems.

Problem Presentation

There are two critical issues involved in presenting the problem. First, if the students are to engage in authentic problem solving, then they must own the problem. We have been learners with the Asteroid Problem and we have been facilitators in two contexts: with a group of high school students and with a group of our peers who were attending a workshop to learn about constructivism. In all three cases, the learners were thoroughly engaged in the problem. Frankly, we were amazed at the generality across these disparate groups. In presenting this problem, we used a 10–minute video that described asteroids and showed the large number of sites on earth where they have hit and the kind of impact they can have (the diamond field in South Africa, the possibility that an asteroid caused the extinction of dinosaurs, Crater Lake, etc.). We also talked about recent near misses—one in Alabama within the last year and one three years ago that could have hit Australia or Russia. Thus, the problem clearly has potential cataclysmic effects (we have past history) and it is a current real problem (we have had near misses quite recently).[4] This step in the PBL process of "bringing the problem home" is critical. The learners must perceive the problem as a real problem and one which has personal relevance. Of course, also central is the fact that the learners have ownership of the problem—they are not just trying to figure out what we want.

A second critical issue in presenting the problem is to be certain that the data presented do not highlight critical factors in the case. Too often when problems are presented, the only information that is provided is the key information relevant to the desired solution (end-of-chapter "problems" are notorious for this). Either the case must be richly presented or present only as a basic question. For example, Honebein, Marrero, Kakos-Kraft, and Duffy (1994) present all of the medical notes on a patient, while Barrows (1985) provides answers generated by the presenting physician to any of 270 questions the learners might ask. In contrast, Milter and Stinson (1994) presented only a four-word question and rely on natural resources to provide the full context.

Facilitator Role

In his discussion of the tutorial process, Barrows states:

> The ability of the tutor to use facilitory teaching skills during the small group learning process is the major determinant of the quality and the success of any educational method aimed at (1) developing students' thinking or reasoning skills (problem solving, metacognition, critical thinking) as they learn, and (2) helping them to become independent, self-directed learners (learning to learn, learning management). Tutoring is a teaching skill central to problem-based, self-directed learning. (1992, p. 12)

Throughout a session, the facilitator models higher order thinking by asking questions which probe students' knowledge deeply. To do this, the facilitator constantly asks "Why?" "What do you mean?" "How do you know that's true?" Barrows is adamant that the facilitators' interactions with the students be at a metacognitive level (except for housekeeping tasks) and that the facilitator avoid expressing an opinion or giving information to the students. The facilitator does not use his or her knowledge of the content to ask questions that will lead the learners to the "correct" answer.

A second tutor role is to challenge the learners' thinking. The facilitator (and hopefully the other students in this collaborative environment) will constantly ask: "Do you know what that means? What are the implications of that? Is there anything else?" Superficial thinking and vague notions do not go unchallenged. During his introduction of the Asteroid Problem, Barrows noted for the group that saying nothing about another member's facts or opinions was the same as saying "I agree." Similarly, the responsibility for a flawed medical diagnosis was shared by everyone in the group. During the first few PBL sessions, the facilitator challenges both the level of understanding and the relevance and completeness of the issues studied. Gradually, however, the students take over this role themselves as they become effective self-directed learners.

> Students are encouraged and expected to think both critically and creatively and to monitor their own understanding . . .

CONCLUSION

Our goal in this article was to present PBL as a detailed instructional model and to show how PBL is consistent with the principles of instruction arising from constructivism. We sought to provide a clear link between theory and practice. Some of the features of the PBL environment are that the learners are actively engaged in working at tasks and activities that are authentic to the environment in which they would be used. The focus is on learners as constructors or their own knowledge in a context similar to that in which they would apply that knowledge. Students are encouraged and expected to think both critically and creatively and to monitor their own understanding, i.e., function at a metacognitive level. Social negotiation of meaning is an important part of the problem-solving team structure and the facts of the case are only facts when the group decides they are.

PBL, as we have described it, contrasts with a variety of other problem or case based approaches. Most case based learning strategies (Williams, 1992) use cases as a means for testing one's understanding. The case is presented after the topic is covered in order to help test understanding and support synthesis. In contrast, in PBL, all of the learning arises out of consideration of the problem. From the start, the learning is synthesized and organized in the context of the problem.

Other case approaches simply use the case as a concrete reference point for learning. Learning objectives and resources are presented along with the case. These approaches use the case as an "example" and are not focused on developing the metacognitive skills associated with problem solving or with professional life. The contrast is perhaps that the PBL approach is a cognitive apprenticeship focusing on both the knowledge domain and the problem solving associated with that knowledge domain or profession. Other problem approaches present cases so that critical attributes are highlighted, thus emphasizing the content domain, but not engaging the learner in authentic problem solving in that domain.

Finally, this is not a Socratic process, nor is it a kind of limited discovery learning environment in which the goal for the learner is to "discover" the outcome the instructor *wants*. The learners have ownership of the problem. The facilitation is not knowledge driven; rather, it is focused on metacognitive processes.

NOTES

1. This succinct statement was noted in Gaffney & Anderson (1991).

2. Let us hasten to add that many simulation environments are not designed to engage the learner in the problems they are addressing. This is a design issue, not a natural component of a particular instructional strategy.

3. PBL students do as well as the traditional students in a variety of discipline areas on standard or Board qualifying exams. The PBL students seem to retain their knowledge longer after the exam than students in traditional classes (Boud & Feletti, 1991; Bridges & Hallinger, 1992).

4. The potential value of real-world problems in terms of sustained learning and potential impact on interest in the news is illustrated in terms of the 1994 collisions of asteroids with Jupiter. Once having engaged in the asteroid "problem," news concerning asteroid events takes on considerably greater significance.

REFERENCES

Barrows, H. S. (1985). *How to design a problem based curriculum of the preclinical years.* New York: Springer Publishing Co.

———. (1986). A taxonomy of problem based learning methods. *Medical Education, 20,* 481–486.

———. (1992). *The tutorial process.* Springfield, IL: Southern Illinois University School of Medicine.

Barrows, H. S., & Myers, A. C. (1993). *Problem based learning in secondary schools.* Unpublished monograph. Springfield, IL: Problem Based Learning Institute, Lanphier High School, and Southern Illinois University Medical School.

Bereiter, C. (1994). Implications of Postmodernism for science, or, science as progressive discourse. *Educational Psychologist, 29,* 3–12.

Blumenfeld, P. C., Soloway, E., Marx, R. W., Krajcik, J. S., Guzdial, M., & Palincsar, A. (1991). Motivating project-based learning: Sustaining the doing, supporting the learning. *Educational Psychologist, 26* (3&4), 369–398.

Boud, D., & Feletti, G. (Eds.) (1991). *The challenge of problem based learning.* New York: St. Martin's Press.

Bridges, E., & Hallinger, P. (1992). *Problem based learning for administrators.* ERIC Clearinghouse on Educational Management, University of Oregon.

Brooks, J. G., & Brooks, M. G. (1993). *In search of understanding: The case for constructivist classrooms.* Alexandria, VA: Association for Supervision and Curriculum Development.

Brown, J. S., Collins, A., & Duguid, P. (1989). Situated cognition and the culture of learning. *Educational Researcher, 18(1),* 32–42.

Clift, R., Houston, W., & Pugach, M. (Eds.), (1990). *Encouraging reflective practice in education.* New York: Teachers College Press.

Cognition & Technology Group at Vanderbilt. (1992). Technology and the design of generative learning environments. In T. M. Duffy & D. H. Jonassen (Eds.), *Constructivism and the technology of instruction: A conversation.* Hillsdale, NJ: Lawrence Erlbaum Associates. Originally in *Educational Technology, 1991, 31*(5).

Cognition & Technology Group at Vanderbilt. (1994). From visual word problems to learning communities: Changing conceptions of cognitive research. In K. McGilly (Ed.), *Classroom lessons: Integrating cognitive theory and classroom practice.* Cambridge, MA: MIT Press/Bradford Brooks.

Cohen, E. (1994). Restructuring the classroom: Conditions for productive small groups. *Review of Educational Research, 64,* 1–35.

Collins, A., Brown, J. S., & Newman, S. E. (1989). Cognitive apprenticeship: Teaching the crafts of reading, writing, and mathematics. In L. B. Resnick (Ed.), *Knowing, learning, and instruction: Essays in honor of Robert Glaser* (pp. 453–494). Hillsdale, NJ: Lawrence Erlbaum Associates.

Cunningham, D. J., Duffy, T. M., & Knuth, R. A. (1991). The textbook of the future. In C. McKnight, A. Dillon, & J. Richardson (Eds.), *Hypertext: A psychological perspective.* London: Horwood Publishing.

Dewey, J. (1938). *Logic: The theory of inquiry.* New York: Holt and Co.

Duffy, T. M. (1994). *Corporate and community education: Achieving success in the information society.* Unpublished paper, Bloomington, IN: Indiana University.

———. (in press). *Strategic teaching frameworks: An instructional model for complex, interactive skills.* To appear in C. Dills & A. Romiszowski, (Eds.), *Instructional development.* Englewood Cliffs, NJ: Educational Technology Publications.

Duffy, T. M., & Jonassen, D. H. (Eds.) (1992). *Constructivism and the technology of instruction: A conversation.* Hillsdale, NJ: Lawrence Erlbaum Associates.

Duffy, T. M., Lowyck, J., & Jonassen, D. H. (Eds.) (1993). *Designing environments for constructivist learning.* Berlin: Springer-Verlag.

Edelson, D., & O'Neil, K. (1994). *The CoVis collaboratory notebook: Computer support for scientific inquiry.* Paper presented at the annual meeting of the American Educational Research Association, New Orleans.

Fosnot, C. T. (1989). *Enquiring teachers, enquiring learners. A Constructivist approach to teaching.* New York: Teachers College Press.

Gaffney, J. S., & Anderson, R. C. (1991). Two-tiered scaffolding: Congruent processes of teaching and learning. In E. H. Hiebert (Ed.), *Literacy for a diverse society: Perspectives, practices, & policies.* New York: Teachers College Press.

Honebein, P., Duffy, T. M., & Fishman, B. (1993). Constructivism and the design of learning environments: Context and authentic activities for learning. In T. M. Duffy, J. Lowyck, & D. H. Jonassen (Eds.), *Designing environments for constructivist learning.* Berlin: Springer-Verlag.

Honebein, P., Marrero, D. G., Kakos-Kraft, S., & Duffy, T. M. (1994). *Improving medical students' skills in the clinical care of diabetes.* Paper presented at the annual meeting of the American Diabetes Association, New Orleans.

Johnson, D. W., & Johnson, R. T., (1990). Cooperative learning and achievement. In S. Sharan (Ed.), *Cooperative learning: Theory and practice.* New York: Praeger.

Kagan, S. (1992). *Cooperative learning.* San Juan Capistrano, CA: Kagan Cooperative Learning.

Lebow, D. (1993). Constructivist values for systems design: Five principles toward a new mindset. *Educational Technology Research and Development, 41,* 4–16.

MacDonald, P. J. (1991). Selection of health problems for a problem-based curriculum. In D. Boud & G. Feletti (Eds.), *The challenge of problem based learning.* New York: St. Martin's Press.

Miller, R. G., & Stinson, J. E. (1994). Educating leaders for the new competitive environment. In G. Gijselaers, S. Tempelaar, & S. Keizer S. (Eds.), *Educational innovation in economics and business administration: The case of problem-based learning.* London: Kluwer Academic Publishers.

Piaget, J. (1977). *The development of thought: Equilibrium of cognitive structures.* New York: Viking Press.

Resnick, L. B. (1987). Learning in school and out. *Educational Researcher, 16,* 13–20.

Rorty, R. (1991). *Objectivity, relativism, and truth.* Cambridge: Cambridge University Press.

Roschelle, J. (1992). *Reflections of Dewey and technology for situated learning.* Paper presented at annual meeting of the American Educational Research Association, San Francisco.

Ruopp, R., Gal, S., Drayton, B., & Pfister, M. (Eds.) (1993). *LabNet: Toward a community of practice.* Hillsdale, NJ: Lawrence Erlbaum Associates.

Scardamalia, M., & Bereiter, C. (1991). Higher levels of agency for children in knowledge building: A challenge for the design of new knowledge media. *The Journal of the Learning Sciences, 1,* 37–68.

Scardamalia, M., Bereiter, C., Brett, C., Burtis, P. J., Calhoun, & Lea, N. S. (1992). Educational applications of a networked communal database. *Interactive Leaning Environments, 2,* 45–71.

Schön, D. A. (1987). *Educating the reflective practitioner.* San Francisco: Jossey-Bass.

Slavin, R. (1990). *Cooperative learning: Theory, research, and practice.* Boston: Allyn and Bacon.

Spiro, R. J., Feltovich, P. L., Jacobson, M. J., & Coulson, R. L. (1992). Cognitive flexibility, constructivism, and hypertext: Random access for advanced knowledge acquisition in illstructured domains. In T. M. Duffy & D. H. Jonassen (Eds.), *Constructivism and the technology of instruction: A conversation.* Hillsdale, NJ: Lawrence Erlbaum Associates. Originally in *Educational Technology,* 1991, *31*(5).

Stinson, J. E. (1994). *Can Digital Equipment survive?* Paper presented at the Sixth International Conference on Thinking, Boston, MA.

Williams, S. M., (1992) Putting case-based instruction into context: Examples from legal and medical education. *Journal of the Learning Sciences, 2,* 367–427.

vonGlasersfeld, E. (1989). Cognition, construction of knowledge, and teaching. *Synthese, 80,* 121–140.

Vygotsky, L. S. (1978) *Mind in Society: The development of higher psychological processes.* Cambridge MA: Harvard University Press.

Section 3

Applications . . . Problem-Based Learning

The message from the moon . . . is that no problem need any longer be considered insoluble.

—Norman Cousins

The applications of problem-based learning (PBL) demonstrate ways in which "passion for learning" is restored to the classroom. Historically, inventors, explorers, scientists, and the creative geniuses of all ages have been intrigued by problems that ignited their interest. PBL as a classroom model is just as engaging to students today as problems were to the great thinkers years ago. In this section, two essays serve to tell the story of PBL in today's classrooms.

Beginning with a practical version of classroom application, Savoie and Hughes discuss their experience with giving students a problem that really connects with their world. They note how this relevant learning empowers students to generate solutions and think seriously about the situations and appropriate, acceptable solutions. They argue that students using PBL come to grips with significant academic subject matter and take their learning beyond the classroom walls into the real world with them. The authors discuss the empowerment of students as learners as students work in small teams and demonstrate their learning, and they suggest further possibilities for classrooms.

While the second article in this section on applications, *Motivating Project-Based Learning: Sustaining the Doing, Supporting the Learning*, by Blumenfeld and others, has "project-based" in the title rather than "problem-based," be assured that the research base and the context of the discussion are inextricably related to the overall discussion of PBL. In this article, the authors argue that projects are motivational to learning, to thinking about that learning, and to really understanding learning. This in-depth discussion looks at a number of factors that lead to motivated and engaged learning, interest and value, perceived and achieved competence, task focus, and the role of technology in enhancing student involvement and addressing problems faced in the project-oriented classroom.

In summary, the articles collected in this section focus on the application issues. They move from guiding the process to classroom solutions and ways to support the process. It is all there for the discerning reader.

Problem-Based Learning as Classroom Solution

by Joan M. Savoie and Andrew S. Hughes

Give students a problem that really connects with their world, empower them to generate solutions, and watch the serious thinking that follows.

Venturing into problem-based learning with everyone's least favorite 9th grade class took us into uncharted waters. Although we were aware of its value in professional teacher education, we knew little about the possibilities of problem-based learning with teenagers. Bolstered by the success reported by Stepien and Gallagher (1993) and supported by a colleague whose 9th grade social studies class agreed to give it a try, we set sail.[1]

In planning our two-week unit, we observed the following characteristics of problem-based learning:

1. Begin with a problem.
2. Ensure that the problem connects with the students' world.
3. Organize the subject matter around the problem, not around the disciplines.
4. Give students the major responsibility for shaping and directing their own learning.
5. Use small teams as the context for most learning.
6. Require students to demonstrate what they have learned through a product or a performance.

BEGIN WITH A PROBLEM

Rather than give over the entire course to problem-based learning, we decided to "post-hole," or insert, a problem into the regular program (Stepien and Gallagher 1993). The course was one in Global Studies; the unit, Tradition and Change; the theme, The Family. The problem came from the classroom edition of the *Wall Street Journal* ("Case Study," 1993):

> You are a marriage counselor with an appointment to meet Betty and Bob Stevens. . . . They have been married seven years. Betty is a regional manager for a health supplies company. She has been promoted three times since she joined the firm; the most recent promotion was about 13 months ago. Bob is a reporter for a local newspaper, who hopes to move to a larger paper after another year or two of experience. The couple has one child, Shawn, age 6.
>
> Bob began seeing a psychologist a year ago after becoming depressed and noticing the number of family arguments had increased. Betty can't identify a specific problem, but feels their marriage has certainly taken a turn for the worse over the past year. How can you help this couple?

CONNECT WITH YOUR STUDENTS' WORLD

The problem selected has two characteristics that we considered essential. First, it is authentic in that it connects to the "larger social context within which the students live" (Newmann and Wehlage 1993). Second, it is rooted in the subject matter of the curriculum; in this case, the study of tradition and change as they affect families.

For us, it was important that the problem address a social issue of historical and contemporary interest. In no way did we want our work to be construed as group counseling or therapy. Problem-based learning is a mechanism for allowing students to come to grips with significant academic subject matter.

After introducing the problem, we divided students into small groups that we thought would work well together. The seven project groups included from two to four members. In grappling with the limited information provided, students disagreed about reasons for the family's problem. Several determined that the couple did not spend enough time together. As one boy heatedly informed his group, "He's a newspaper reporter. They have to chase the news wherever it is." Others were convinced it was a simple matter of jealousy: Bob envied his wife's success. And, without any tangible information, several students pegged 6-year-old Shawn as the source of the problem.

At the end of the first class period, students compiled a list of questions that they would like to ask the Stevenses:

- What do you argue about?
- How much time do you spend together alone?
- Are you still in love?
- Do your arguments concern Shawn? Is he afraid when you argue?
- How much money do you each make?

During the next class, we had intended to spend only a few minutes listening to students justifying their choices, but nearly a half hour later, hands were still waving for the chance to share one last question.

Next, we introduced a three-step problem-solving process suggested by Stepien, Gallagher, and Workman (1993): What do we know? What do we need to know? What are we going to do? In addition to serving as an instructional scaffold from which students might make sense of the situation, the questions enabled us to help them separate facts from value judgments, speculate about causes and effects, evaluate possible actions, and the like.

The students were attentive, active participants. Later, when asked how the class members had demonstrated effort, one girl replied, "We thought!" As teachers, however, we ended the day dissatisfied. We had succumbed to the tyranny of time, urging students to move along before they were fully ready. In retrospect, it occurred to us that: (1) breaking the school day into six or seven 45-minute periods is not conductive to in-depth discussions; and (2) facilitating the problem-solving process requires honing our skill in asking questions and probing students' responses.

ORGANIZE SUBJECT MATTER AROUND THE PROBLEM

In problem-based learning, the purpose of the problem is to motivate students to learn and provide a real-world context for examining the issues involved. Certainly, the initial brainstorming evoked enthusiasm and speculation, but little enlightenment. Providing students with a range of learning resources, we hoped, would enable them to shed more light on the problem.

First, we distributed written materials about such concepts as equity, sharing, responsibility, and the "trailing response" (the one who lags behind in status and money in a two-career family)—as well as statistical profiles of dual-earner families. We also provided students with the following additional information about the Stevenses:

- Betty has the larger salary and is in line for promotion to the national office.
- Bob's current job offers no opportunity for advancement, and he has not received any responses to resumes that he has sent out.
- They have a new house with a big mortgage.
- Betty is extremely active in community affairs during her spare time ("Case Study," 1993).

After we introduced these details, the students were quick to recognize that Betty seemed to hold all the power. As one girl summed it up:

> Betty has the big job, makes the most money, drives the best car, does all the traveling, and is out all the time. Bob stays home, minds Shawn, and is depressed.

In their discussion, students called upon a broad range of information, not just from the case description but from their personal experiences as well. Surely these were not the same students who struggled to remember even the simplest information in their regular social studies classes.

Second, we invited a psychologist and a counselor to the classroom to discuss their jobs in general and reflect about the Stevens's situation, in particular. To prepare for the psychologist's visit, each group answered questions on a visitor focus sheet: who is coming and why, how is the visitor important to us, and what do we want to tell her and ask about the problem (Center for Gifted Education 1993).

Although we often invite visitors to our classrooms, this time students and visitor were linked by common ground. The students recognized and were eager to benefit from the psychologist's experience and expertise. They asked how she viewed the problem and what she would suggest. They discussed depression and its many forms. They also raised questions about her own work in schools: "Did you ever deal with suicide?" "Is it hard not to let your emotions get involved?"

The counselor's visit went equally well. In fact, several weeks later, students still referred to the "full balloon," an analogy the counselor used to describe feelings. When he named the location of his feelings (his balloon) as being in his chest and stomach, several students jumped in and added "throat and knees" as places where they often sense feelings. The counselor suggested that Bob Stevens's balloon was so full (his feelings were so overwhelming) that it would be hard for him to address the problem until he could "deflate the balloon." One student blurted out, "We have to collapse the balloon and not him." We were talking about the Stevenses, but the students were thinking about themselves.

EMPOWER STUDENTS AS LEARNERS

One of the dilemmas we faced with problem-based learning was that, obviously, our students were not totally responsible for directing their own learning. After all, we selected the problem and the initial learning resources. Still, within the confines of the general problem, students set a learning agenda and decided how to pursue it. Some chose to probe the sources of stress in family life; others examined changing family structures; still others compiled statistics on two-earner families. The resources we provided served only as springboards to lift students from simplistic reactions to more complex conversations and conclusions about how the changing roles of men and women can affect modern family life.

> Later, many of the students told us that they had shared the problem and their responses to it with parents and friends.

Later, many of the students told us that they had shared the problem and their responses to it with parents and friends. Obviously, they were checking out their own thinking, seeking affirmation. Clearly, this problem had struck a chord.

USE SMALL TEAMS FOR MOST LEARNING

While the small team was not the only learning forum in our problem-based learning unit, it was the main one. We assembled the whole class for the two visitors and, from time to time, gathered as a class to debrief the work done to that point.

This particular class had not had much experience working in small groups. Would students listen to, and show appreciation for, one another's contributions? Would they stay on task? Would they share responsibility for a group product? No doubt students need important skills to work effectively in groups, but we suspect that, in the context of the total learning environment, these skills are considerably less important than a good problem. One student's comment seemed to summarize the prevailing feeling about the small group discussions:

> Everyone's learning together. . . . If someone doesn't understand, you're in a group. I mean they'll usually explain it to you more. No one's left out. Everyone gets the message and gets what you're doing.

HAVE STUDENTS DEMONSTRATE THEIR LEARNING

From the outset, we told students that they would be required to demonstrate what they had learned about the changing nature of family life. Specifically, each group had two choices. They could compose a letter to the Stevenses, offering advice based on what they had learned during the project, or individual students could play the role of a marriage counselor in a meeting with the couple. When our original plan to have a married couple act the part of Bob and Betty went awry, we asked for volunteers to role-play the troubled couple. Of those who offered, three, according to the regular teacher, had previously been unwilling to participate in any sort of role-playing activity.

How did the students do? In demonstrating their learning, they revealed a seriousness of purpose; a knowledge of relevant social concepts (such as spousal and parental responsibilities, gender issues, sharing and compromise); and, intriguingly, some knowledge of, and interest in, the skills of counseling.

WHAT DID *WE* LEARN?

To be sure, problem-based learning was a change of pace—but was it anything else? What are the standards by which we can judge it?

The five standards for authentic instruction suggested by Newmann and Wehlage (1993) are an excellent place to begin: Is the emphasis upon higher-order thinking? Is the stress upon in-depth knowledge? Is the subject matter closely connected to questions of the human condition? Is the inquiry focused and coherent? Are teachers and students committed to mutual respect, strong effort, and good performance?

Our sense is that the approach helps to shape the learning environment around these standards of authentic instruction. We observed highly motivated, engaged young people eager to share their thoughts about the problem, both inside and outside of the classroom. One student wondered, "So what do you teachers think of this way of teaching?" and then immediately answered her own question: "This way you get to know your students better. You get to make sure they know what they're doing. You know if they understand."

If this is what problem-based learning can look like with a challenging 9th grade class and teachers inexperienced with the approach, we wonder what its other possibilities might be.

NOTES

1. Joan Savoie and the regular classroom teacher tutored the class in problem-based learning. Andrew Hughes helped plan the unit and interviewed the students about the experience. Both authors are involved in a larger project assessing the value of problem-based learning in university and school settings.

2. The case study section of the *Wall Street Journal*'s monthly classroom edition provides wonderful sample problems and advice about using them.

REFERENCES

"Case Study." (May 1993). *Wall Street Journal Classroom Edition:* 23.

Center for Gifted Education. (1993). *Hot Rods: Nuclear Energy and Nuclear Waste.* Williamsburg, Va.: The College of William and Mary.

Newmann, F. M., and G. G. Wehlage. (1993). "Five Standards of Authentic Instruction." *Educational Leadership* 50, 7: 8–12.

Stepien, W., and S. Gallagher. (1993). "Problem-Based Learning: As Authentic As It Gets." *Educational Leadership* 50, 7: 25–28.

Stepien, W., S. Gallagher, and D. Workman. (1993). "Problem-Based Learning for Traditional and Interdisciplinary Classrooms." *Journal for the Education of the Gifted* 16, 4: 338–357.

Motivating Project-Based Learning: Sustaining the Doing, Supporting the Learning

by Phyllis C. Blumenfeld, Elliot Soloway, Ronald W. Marx, Joseph S. Krajcik, Mark Guzdial, and Annemarie Palincsar
The University of Michigan

Project-based learning is a comprehensive approach to classroom teaching and learning that is designed to engage students in investigation of authentic problems. In this article, we present an argument for why projects have the potential to help people learn; indicate factors in project design that affect motivation and thought; examine difficulties that students and teachers may encounter with projects; and describe how technology can support students and teachers as they work on projects, so that motivation and thought are sustained.

How can I motivate children? How can I get children to think about what they are doing, not just focus on getting it done? How can I get children to really understand the material, not just pass tests? These are age-old and important questions of educators and continue to be central issues in psychological research. Motivational questions are often studied in isolation from questions of thinking and learning; however, the job of the teacher requires an integration of these two related, but often disparate, areas of study. If one of the important goals of schooling is to foster the development of students' minds by engaging them in sophisticated and substantial opportunities for deep understanding of curricular content, then educators must concern themselves with motivational questions that examine how students engage in and persist at such activities.

In searching for organizing principles of instruction and curriculum that attend to critical relations between motivation and thinking, researchers have recurrently turned to the idea of projects:

From *Educational Psychologist,* 26(3 & 4), pp. 369–398. Copyright © 1991, Lawrence Erlbaum Associates, Inc. Reprinted with permission.

relatively long-term, problem-focused, and meaningful units of instruction that integrate concepts from a number of disciplines or fields of study. In this article, we present an argument for why projects have the potential to help people learn; indicate factors in project design that affect motivation and thought; examine difficulties that students and teachers may encounter with projects; and describe how technology can support students and teachers as they work on projects, so that motivation and thought are sustained.

Within the last decade, a considerable body of empirical research and theory has shown the link between student motivational orientation and cognitive engagement in schoolwork (Ames & Archer, 1988; Dweck & Elliot, 1983; Harter, 1983; Meece, Blumenfeld, & Hoyle, 1988; Nolen, 1988; Pintrich & De Groot, 1990; Pokay & Blumenfeld, 1990; Winne & Marx, 1989). Several sets of goal orientations have been proposed: mastery versus ability, learning versus performance, and task versus ego involvement. Each set of goals differs primarily in terms of whether learning is perceived and valued as an end in itself or as a means to external ends such as grades, gaining approval, or avoiding negative evaluation by others. Students who adopt goals characteristic of the first of each of the pairs are motivated to learn (Brophy, 1983). Such students try to benefit from school assignments and demonstrate greater levels of cognitive engagement in schoolwork, and they report using more self-regulation, cognitive, and metacognitive strategies. Use of such strategies is related to the development of deeper level understanding of subject content (Weinstein & Mayer, 1986; Wittrock, 1986).

> Within the last decade, a considerable body of empirical research and theory has shown the link between student motivational orientation and cognitive engagement in schoolwork.

In addition to stressing the importance of learning strategies, recent work on learning emphasizes the critical role played by tasks and the environment. Previous work on tasks suggests that they serve as critical links among student motivation, student cognition, instruction, and learning (Bennett, DesForges, Cockburn, & Wilkinson, 1984; Blumenfeld, Mergendoller, & Swarthout, 1987; Doyle, 1983; Marx & Walsh, 1988). In fact, tasks have been described as the basic instructional unit in classrooms. Those who have characterized instructional tasks express dismay about the focus on low-level facts and skills and the omnipresence of worksheets in American classrooms (e.g., C. W. Anderson & Smith, 1987; Brophy & Alleman, 1991; Doyle, 1983; Sizer, 1984). Students are afforded few opportunities to represent knowledge in a variety of ways, pose and solve real problems, or use their knowledge to create artifacts.[1] The prevalence of low-level tasks contributes to students' lack of understanding of content and process and poor attitudes toward learning and schooling.

The introduction of more cognitively complex tasks, which provide opportunities for solving real problems, often is urged as a remedy for this situation. Drawing analogies from everyday learning, researchers argue that knowledge is contexualized; that is, learners construct knowledge by solving complex problems in situations in which they use cognitive tools, multiple sources of information, and other individuals as resources (Brown, Collins, & Duguid, 1989; Resnick, 1987). Moreover, because learning occurs in a social context, learners interact with and internalize modes of knowing and thinking represented and practiced in a community (Toulmin, 1972). The master-apprentice relationship is used as an analogy for the teaching-learning situation. It is argued that, like masters, teachers should scaffold instruction by breaking down tasks; use modeling, promoting, and coaching to teach strategies for thinking and problem solving; and gradually release responsibility to the learner. The result of such an approach to teaching is that learners are motivated to persist at authentic problems, meld prior knowledge and experience with new leaning, and develop rich domain-specific knowledge and thinking strategies to apply to real-world problems.

PROJECT-BASED LEARNING AS MOTIVATIONAL

An integrative perspective on motivation and learning has led to new interest in student projects. Project-based learning is a comprehensive perspective focused on teaching by engaging students in investigation. Within this framework, students pursue solutions to nontrivial problems by asking and refining questions, debating ideas, making predictions, designing plans and/or experiments, collecting and analyzing data, drawing conclusions, communicating their ideas and findings to others, asking new questions, and creating artifacts.

There are two essential components of projects: They require a question or problem that serves to organize and drive activities; and

these activities result in a series of artifacts, or products, that culmi-
nate in a final product that addresses the driving question. Students
can be responsible for the creation of both the
question and the activities, as well as the
nature of the artifacts. In addition, teachers
or curriculum developers can create questions
and activities. However, in neither case can
the question be so constrained that the outcomes are predetermined, leaving students
with little room to develop their own
approaches to answering the question. Students' freedom to generate artifacts is critical,
because it is through this process of generation that students construct their knowledge—
the doing and the learning are inextricable. Artifacts are representations of the students' problem solutions that reflect emergent states
of knowledge. Because artifacts are concrete and explicit (e.g., a
model, report, videotape, or computer program) they can be shared
and critiqued. This allows others to provide feedback and permits
learners to reflect on and extend their emergent knowledge and
revise their artifacts.

> **Projects are decidely different from conventional activities that are designed to help students learn information in the absence of a driving question.**

Projects are decidedly different from conventional activities that
are designed to help students learn information in the absence of a
driving question. Such conventional activities might relate to each
other and help students learn curricular content, but, without the
presence of a driving question, they do not hold the same promise
that learning will occur as do activities orchestrated in the service of
an important intellectual purpose (e.g., Sizer, 1984). Proponents of
project-based learning claim that as students investigate and seek
resolutions to problems, they acquire an understanding of key principles and concepts. Project-based learning also places students in
realistic, contextualized problem-solving environments. In so doing,
projects can serve to build bridges between phenomena in the classroom and real-life experiences; the questions and answers that arise
in their daily enterprise are given value and are shown to be open to
systematic inquiry. Hence, project-based education requires active
engagement of students' efforts over an extended period of time.
Project-based learning also promotes links among subject matter.
Finally, projects are adaptable to different types of learners and
learning situations.

Examples of published projects include those produced by the Technical Education Research Center and the National Geographic Society on science topics including acid rain and solar energy. These particular projects focus on important environmental problems (although there is no reason why projects need to focus on applied issues); involve students in data gathering and analysis; examine local industry and laws; and make use of new technologies, including microcomputer packages and telecommunications, with which students can gain information as well as share their findings with others outside the classroom. Similar projects built on a smaller scale can be developed by classroom teachers or teams of teachers. Whether the project is developed by publishers, teachers, or students, activities associated with these projects should be designed to be interesting and meaningful to learners and promote a deep level understanding of the content.

PROBLEMS WITH PROJECT-BASED LEARNING AND SOURCES OF SOLUTIONS

There is a richness to a good project that can be exploited by teachers and students. Projects can increase student interest because they involve students in solving authentic problems, in working with others, and in building real solutions (artifacts). Projects have the potential to enhance deep understanding because students need to acquire and apply information, concepts, and principles, and they have the potential to improve competence in thinking (learning and metacognition) because students need to formulate plans, track progress, and evaluate solutions.

Despite considerable potential, project-based education is not without problems. The idea that projects represent learning by doing certainly is not new. Roots of this conception go back to Dewey. However, lessons from the past suggest that without adequate attention to ways of supporting teachers and students, these innovative educational approaches will not be widely adopted. Previous attempts at reform of curriculum and instruction in the 1960s used "hands-on" and discovery learning as central themes. Although evidence suggests that such curricula enhanced student learning and motivation (e.g., Bredderman, 1983), their adoption was not as widespread as desired. Many reasons can be advanced for this. We submit that the projects were developed and disseminated without sufficient appreciation for the complex nature of student motivation and knowledge required to engage in cognitively difficult work. Furthermore, there was little regard for considering questions from the point of view of students (as distinguished from experts). Finally, little attention was paid to the nature and extent of teacher knowledge and commitment and the complexity of classroom organization.

The newer cognitively based approaches that contemporary projects represent also require substantial changes in teachers' thinking about and dispositions toward classroom structures, activities, and tasks. These changes, as previous curriculum innovations have demonstrated, are not easy to achieve. A quarter of a century of research and development has suggested that innovation in curriculum and instructional practice requires that considerable attention be paid to curricular content and organization, psychological factors associated with learners (e.g., individual and developmental differences in use of knowledge, motivational orientation, cognitive strategies, and metacognition), and professional practice issues of teachers (e.g., teacher efficacy, opportunities for professional development with colleagues, and organizational time and support for teacher reflection). In order to realize the potential of project-based instruction, projects must be designed that sustain student motivation and thoughtfulness and teachers must be supported in creating this type of instruction. Close attention, then, must be given to the design of project question and associated activities and to strategies to improve teachers' implementation of projects.

> In order to realize the potential of project-based instruction, projects must be designed that sustain student motivation and thoughtfulness . . .

One of the major educational developments in the past quarter of a century that has potential for fostering project-based education is the creation and expansion of new educational technology tools that can support students and teachers in obtaining, analyzing, and sharing information and constructing artifacts. Technological power is advancing rapidly. Prices are falling, making sophisticated options affordable for schools. Technology has the potential to sustain student motivation and support student learning and doing during the various phases of projects. It can support teachers in similar ways. Technology can supplement and complement teachers' instructional and managerial roles, relieving teachers of some of the complexities of implementing projects. It also can help sustain teacher involvement in project-based education by enhancing their knowledge and professional competence.

In the next sections, we review work on students' motivation and learning, teachers, and technology. We discuss what prior research has established, describe some of the work under way by our group and others, and note the problems that need to be addressed in developing and implementing project-based education.

THE ROLE OF PROJECT DESIGN IN ENHANCING MOTIVATION AND FOSTERING COGNITIVE ENGAGEMENT

To benefit from project-based instruction, students need to be cognitively engaged with subject matter over an extended period of time. Advocates of a focus on complex tasks as an important component of classroom instruction assume that students will be motivated to test their ideas and deepen their understanding when confronted by authentic problems in a situation that is similar to how learning occurs in out-of-school settings. Unfortunately, evidence indicates that students do not necessarily respond to high-level tasks with increased use of learning strategies (C. W. Anderson & Roth, 1989; Blumenfeld & Meece, 1988; Winne & Marx, 1982). Students often are resistant to tasks that involve high-level cognitive processing and try to simplify the demands of the situation through negotiation (Doyle, 1983; Stake & Easley, 1978). Although students may be interested in the topic and possess relevant knowledge and procedures for solving problems or mastering new material, they do not necessarily use these strategies (Paris, Lipson, & Wixson, 1983; Winne & Marx, 1982). It is insufficient merely to provide students with opportunities designed to promote knowledge that is integrated, dynamic, and generative, if students will not invest the effort necessary to acquire information, generate and test solutions, and evaluate their findings. Also, complex high-level activities are often implemented by teachers in a manner that reduces the need for student thought (e.g., Blumenfeld, in press; Doyle, 1983). Consequently, project-based education is not likely to work unless projects are designed in such a way that, with teacher support, they marshal, generate, and sustain student motivation and thoughtfulness.

A number of factors should be considered in project design that affect whether students will be motivated to do projects in a manner that fosters understanding. These factors include whether students find the project to be interesting and valuable, whether they perceive that they have the competence to engage in and complete the project, and whether they focus on leaning rather than on outcomes and grades. Although there certainly are individual difference that influence what students find interesting and valuable (Dweck & Elliot, 1983; Harter, 1983; Meece et al., 1988; Nicholls, Patashnick, & Nolen, 1985; Pintrich & De Groot, 1990), we can explore how projects might be designed to increase the likelihood that most students will be motivated by them. We shall review elements of project design that are likely to affect interest and value, perceived and achieved competence, and task focus, and we raise questions for research on these elements.

Interest and Value

The interest and value students attribute to the problem and elements in projects will affect how motivated they will be to engage in the project. Student interest and perceived value are enhanced when (a) tasks are varied and include novel elements; (b) the problem is authentic and has value; (c) the problem is challenging; (d) there is closure, so that an artifact is created; (e) there is choice about what and/or how work is done; and (f) there are opportunities to work with others (Malone & Lepper, 1987). Each of these factors, and how it should be considered in designing projects, is discussed next.

With respect to variety and novelty, there is danger that interest may be heightened at the expense of cognitive engagement. Students may get hooked by dramatic or unique elements in tasks, but such characteristics may not sustain motivation and cognitive engagement over the extended time needed for project-based learning. Instructional activities that resemble entertainment programming on commercial television, might suggest to learners that the medium requires passive rather than active cognitive engagement (Salomon, 1983). In addition, too many "bells and whistles" may deflect focus from the main idea, resulting in confusion among learners regarding the intellectual focus of activities (Winne & Marx, 1982).

Although interest and value are likely to be enhanced by pursuing authentic questions to which students can relate, such as topics dealing with personal health and welfare, community concerns, or current events, we have little systematic empirical information about what problems students actually find valuable, interesting, or useful enough to work on for long periods. Teachers and curriculum designers can gain formation from students' leisure pursuits, but integrating these with academic subject matter remains problematic. In particular, a crucial issue is how to ensure that the project questions are educationally rich enough that in seeking answers students must gain understanding of significant subject matter concepts.

Tasks that have closure and that entail the production of authentic artifacts are more likely to sustain interest. Nevertheless, how to create conditions in which the questions students pursue and the artifacts they produce are not "school like" remains an issue (Malone & Lepper, 1987). Projects also need to be feasible and manageable given the time and resources available to students and teachers (see Brophy & Alleman, 1991). Moreover, artifacts should be rich enough to promote both depth and breadth of knowledge in their creation as well as demonstrate student mastery of the content. The importance of the nature of the artifact cannot be overstated. Artifacts need to require the student to integrate information and use complex thought. If students pursue a problem that promotes complex learning and thinking, but design an artifact that is trivial, the potential benefits of project-based learning are not likely to accrue.

> **The interest and value students attribute to the problem and elements in projects will affect how motivated they will be . . .**

Concerning finding an optimal level of challenge, students are often willing to exert what they consider to be reasonable effort to gain success (Brophy, 1983). However, as the task becomes more difficult or time consuming, students may focus simply on completing the work with minimum effort rather than engaging demanding strategies to try to understand it. Thus, questions remain about how to promote effort and persistence over the extended time necessary to complete projects. Likely areas for research include goal setting, providing opportunities for feedback to encourage continuing work, and building social norms for group work.

A number of researchers (e.g., Deci & Ryan, 1987; Lepper, 1988) have argued that choice and control are critical to enhance motivation to work on classroom tasks. Project design can allow students to exercise choice and control regarding what to work on, how to work, and what products to generate. For instance, students can (a) select project questions, activities, and artifacts; (b) determine how to approach the problem, what steps to follow, what resources to use, and how to allocate responsibility; and (c) choose the artifacts to construct and how to construct them. Balancing students' need for choice and control in the selection of problem questions, approaches, and artifacts so that they feel "ownership" with the need to have students address and learn content defined by curricular mandates and requirements poses a significant dilemma. Moreover, questions abound regarding optimal proportioning of choice and control between teachers and students so that novices are not over-whelmed by the demands of doing projects and select artifacts that facilitate the development and demonstration of subject matter understanding.

A cornerstone of the newer approaches to learning is collabora-tion with students in the same classroom and in classrooms located at other sites. Carefully designed cooperative learning programs have been shown to enhance student achievement and attitudes (e.g., Bossert, 1989; Cohen, 1986; Slavin, 1983). However, group work can diminish thoughtfulness by encouraging reliance on others as resources, thereby decreasing per-sonal responsibility and independent thinking (Corno & Mandinach, 1983). Blumenfeld (in press) found that students reported more motivation to learn but less use of learning and metacognitive strate-gies during small-group work. The learning effectiveness of such organizational arrangement depends largely on the types of prob-lems posed, the way groups are learning (Good, McCaslin, & Reyes, in press; Slavin, 1983; Webb, 1982). Moreover, although they may find the situation enjoyable, students may not have the skills to benefit from collaborative work. Working with others requires that students be able to discuss ideas, communicate clearly, consider alternatives systematically, monitor their own understanding, com-pare their point of view with that of others, and ask clear questions. Such self-directed learning requires considerable cognitive and metacognitive sophistication. Whether students have such sophisti-cation, and how we can help them develop or use it to enhance col-laborative learning is of central importance (cf. Eichinger, Anderson, Palincsar, & David, 1991).

> Carefully designed cooperative learning programs have been shown to enhance student achievement and attitudes.

We have discussed in this section features of project design that are likely to influence student motivation and raised questions that can serve as a research agenda. Questions about features likely to affect interest and value include the following: What projects that entail important subject matter content will students find interesting, challenging, and valuable enough to work on for long periods? What individual differences are likely to influence the ways in which students approach tasks and the resources that they can bring to bear on their work? How do students' self-perceptions of ability and their interests in particular subject areas influence their persistence at difficult tasks as well as their willingness to defer to others when the level of challenge exceeds their capacity to respond? How can we balance students' choice and control over selection of the subject, the approach to the problem, and the artifacts generated while at the same time providing enough structure so that novices won't be overwhelmed? How can we use collaborative work and ensure productive interaction among students?

Perceived and Achieved Competence

In doing projects, students need access to information and examples or representations that will help them to understand and use central ideas. They also need to use tool skills that are necessary to undertake the project (e.g., reading maps, using a compass, or operating computer software). Students need to use an array of learning, metacognitive, and problem-solving strategies during projects. Moreover, they need to keep track of the process and components, because they are likely to go through several iterations of these processes to improve their work Finally, they need to see errors and false steps as learning opportunities rather than as indicators of low ability.

Given these requirements, several factors may affect students' perceived and actual competence as they engage in complex projects. First, students need to have sufficient knowledge of the content and specific skills to explore information pertinent to the problem. Students often have considerable gaps in their knowledge or hold initial preconceptions of fields like mathematics and science that are quite resistant to change. These may interfere with their ability to understand or benefit from information accessed during project-based leaning activities (e.g., Confrey, 1990; Driver & Oldham, 1986).

Second, as we describe in detail in the section entitled The Role of Technology, students need to be proficient at using cognitive tools like computers and accompanying software programs. In any long-term complicated endeavor like project-based learning, students may become discouraged or frustrated if they lack the necessary knowledge and skills, the problem becomes too complex, or the solution is too difficult to determine or demonstrate. The cognitive tools afforded by new technology should support complex learning. However, technology will not be appropriated by students as tools if they believe it is of limited usefulness or too difficult to learn.

Third, students need to be proficient in using cognitive and metacognitive skills to generate plans, systematically make and test predictions, interpret evidence in light of those predictions, and determine solutions. According to Winne and Marx (1990), the elements of these cognitive skills include storing information in memory, monitoring progress toward goals, assembling units of information into larger schemes, rehearsing newly consolidated learning, and translating information from one form of representation to another (e.g., visual to verbal or mathematical to linguistic). Cognitive skills such as these enable students to manage complexity. As the number of ideas to consider or the number of procedures that need to be followed increases, students may need to stay organized, track their progress, and maintain a focus on the problem rather than get confused by its elements. For instance, studies of laboratory work in science (Hofstein & Lunetta, 1982) suggest that students often concentrate more on figuring out how to cope with the procedures than on what they are supposed to learn.

There are at least two types of metacognition that are employed in project-based learning. One is tactical, relating to the moment-to-moment control and regulation of cognition. The other is strategic and concerns more molar levels of control over larger units of thought. These two features of metacognition refer to different types of knowledge about academic tasks. Tactical control represents students' ability to monitor and fine tune thought as they work through the details of particular tasks. This type of cognitive control enables students to remain focused on the goals of the activity while they struggle through the hard work of creating intermediate artifacts. Students who have inadequate tactical control are likely to have difficulty sustaining mental effort in the moment-to-moment work of generating artifacts. Strategic control represents students' ability to engage in purposeful thought over what might seem to be disconnected elements of projects. In project-based learning, students need to be far more responsible for guiding and controlling their own activities and focusing their work on creation of their artifacts over a long period of time. The capability of students to organize their mental effort in the service to these long term purposes depends on strategic metacognition.

Fourth, students' perceptions of the role of errors in fostering learning need to be considered. Errors are detrimental to learning when they are construed as representing failure to learn. But when they are perceived as attempts to make meaning and to solve difficult and demanding problems, then errors signal just those cognitive and motivational efforts that are desirable for project-based education. In fact, errors are a natural and inevitable consequence of working on potentially ambiguous and ambitious tasks. In this vein, Rohrkemper and Corno (1988) argued that leaning to deal with errors is adaptive and can contribute to academic success. Thus, a redefinition of error making is central to success with projects; teachers and students who conceive of errors only as failure to learn will have extraordinary difficulties succeeding at project-based learning.

> ... students need to be far more responsible for guiding and controlling their own activities ...

Project-based leaning requires considerable content and metacognitive knowledge on the part of students as they work on extended and potentially ambiguous activities. Even if they think they can successfully complete the task, students are likely to become frustrated and fail to persist or engage cognitively with the material if they cannot do the task. It is imperative that project design and implementation take account of the difficulties discussed in this section in order to support students' cognitive competence, contribute to their success, and thus sustain their perceived competence.

Questions about features likely to affect perceived competence include the following: How should students' prior knowledge be considered when designing projects and activities for representing key ideas so that students will be able to understand the material and develop competence? How should projects be designed to encourage the use of cognitive and metacognitive skills to develop learning skills and metacognitive abilities? How can projects be designed to help students maintain mastery goals, take risks, and view errors as a natural part of learning in situations in which evaluation and grades are inherent? Obviously, features of project design are not the only factors that will affect student motivation; teachers play a considerable part in whether students will be interested in and believe themselves capable of doing projects. Therefore, we discuss in the next section how teachers can contribute to student motivation and problems teachers may encounter.

Task Focus

Classroom conditions will affect whether students adopt learning or performance goals in doing projects. Even if they are interested in the problem and perceive themselves to be competent to carry out the project, students may not engage the topic in a manner that promotes understanding if the teacher makes performance orientations salient. Performance, rather than learning, orientations are more likely when teachers emphasize grades and comparative performance, discourage risk taking, use evaluation criteria that stress right answers, enforce accountability for work by imposing externally controlling events such as rewards and punishments, or assign primarily low-level tasks. There are many things teachers can do to promote adoption of "mastery" goals (see Maehr & Midgley, this issue). Nevertheless, even in supportive classroom environments, projects still can create anxieties for students that are difficult to dispel. Given the realities of the performance-grade exchange and the fact that tasks such as those in projects are complex and inherently ambiguous and risky (see Doyle, 1983), students are likely to worry about evaluation and may be quite uncertain about what counts as an acceptable artifact.

THE ROLE OF TEACHERS IN ENHANCING MOTIVATION AND FOSTERING COGNITIVE ENGAGEMENT

In project-based education, as in traditional instruction, teachers need to (a) create opportunities for learning by providing access to information; (b) support learning by scaffolding instruction and modeling and guiding students to make tasks more manageable; (c) encourage students to use learning and metacognitive processes; and (d) assess progress, diagnose problems, provide feedback, and evaluate overall results. In addition, teachers need to create an environment conducive to constructive inquiry and manage the classroom to ensure that work is accomplished in an orderly and efficient fashion. In project-based instruction, these issues become more problematic because of the ambiguity of project-based learning, and the likelihood that numerous activities will occur simultaneously, therefore changing classroom management routines and participant structures.

Even well-designed projects cannot sustain student motivation themselves; teachers play a critical role. A central issue is to determine how teachers can help students work through projects in a manner that sustains motivation and thought. No less important is how we can motivate teachers to create and implement project-based learning. Like students, teachers need to feel competent and value what they are doing in order to be willing to engage in new forms of instruction.

> In addition, teachers need to create an environment conducive to constructive inquiry ...

Currently, a great deal of research is being conducted to determine how teachers can best fulfill these roles. Earlier studies focused primarily on how teachers could present information effectively (Rosenshine & Stevens, 1986) or directly teach learning and thinking skills (e.g., Rosenshine, 1987; Weinstein & Mayer, 1986). This knowledge transmission model of teaching has given way to a knowledge transformation conception of teaching. A more contemporary question concerns how teachers can help students examine and expand their own ideas to develop flexible and meaningful understanding of subject matter and modes of thought. Research in the fields of mathematics, science, social studies, and literacy provides models of how such instruction can be accomplished (see Brophy, 1989).

Motivation research also has implications for teacher practices. The focus has moved from concentrating on individual differences to examining how the classroom environment and teacher practices affect the learning goals that students adopt (Ames & Archer, 1988; Corno & Rohrkemper, 1985; Meece, Blumenfeld, & Puro, 1989). Teachers can create environments that promote motivation to learn and encourage inquiry, risk taking, and thoughtfulness by minimizing ability-related information and focusing on learning, not performance. This work has shown that motivation and instruction are intertwined; creating motivation to learn by enhancing interest and value does not necessarily translate into greater cognitive engagement unless teachers also employ instructional practices that press for active learning on the part of students and hold students accountable for understanding (Blumenfeld, in press; Blumenfeld, Puro, & Mergendoller, in press).

Nevertheless, teachers need a great deal of support in carrying out these roles. It is likely that many teachers will have difficulty fulfilling these functions because of their knowledge and beliefs about learning and teaching; instruction that relies heavily on textbooks and worksheet drill and practice; classroom management routines that are based on lock-step scheduling and whole-class activities; and assessment and accountability practices that focus on fact retention, are highly public, and require competitive reward systems. We review some of the problems likely to be encountered before detailing how technology can support students and teachers. We argue that it is not only the student's motivation that must be sustained, but also the teacher's.

> Project-based instruction affords exciting opportunities for teachers and students to explore problems in depth and to draw on concepts across subjects.

Teacher's Content Knowledge, Pedagogical Content Knowledge, and Beliefs

Project-based instruction affords exciting opportunities for teachers and students to explore problems in depth and to draw on concepts across subjects. However, these opportunities assume that teachers possess knowledge of content included in projects, understand how to explain or illustrate content and teach learning strategies, and hold belief systems compatible with a constructivist approach to teaching and learning. These requirements are not easily met.

Like their students, some teachers hold alternative or incomplete conceptions of subject matter (Krajcik & Layman, 1989; Smith & Neale, 1989). Their knowledge of the concepts and the process skills addressed by a project may not be sufficient to enable them to distill the concepts the project addresses, identify possible links between the central ideas in the project and other concepts in the subject area covered in the curriculum, or recognize ways other disciplines can be incorporated into projects. One issue in doing projects is how to help teachers understand project content to enable them to help students.

Teachers may have sufficient understanding of the concepts, but may not have pedagogical content knowledge of probable alternatives; possible misconceptions of students; or activities, explanations, demonstrations, and analogies that can provide powerful illustrations of the concepts (Shulman, 1986). Also, they may not be adept at modeling thinking and problem-solving strategies or scaffolding instruction in ways that progressively release responsibilities to students.

Teachers' beliefs regarding their role, the goals of schooling, and how students learn are frequently antithetical to the assumptions underlying project-based instructional approaches (L. Anderson, 1989). Teachers often view learning as a process of obtaining information rather than an active process of knowledge construction; they often view motivation simply as a problem of developing positive attitudes rather than enhancing cognitive engagement. Thus, they often select tasks with the goal of providing something interesting for students to do and give less attention to achieving cognitive goals, integrating material with prior learning, or considering how the artifacts that students generate influence their thinking and learning (Clark & Peterson, 1986; Shavelson & Stern, 1981; Winne & Marx, 1987).

Instruction

To successfully implement project-based instruction, teachers need to help students become aware of and examine their own conceptions, and develop and use learning strategies. Research over the last decade has identified instructional strategies such as predictions (Lewis & Linn, 1989) and discrepant events (Nussbaum & Novick, 1982; Osborne & Freyberg, 1985) that help make student understanding more explicit. Considerable research in classrooms indicates that carrying out this type of instruction is difficult. Even if teachers are sympathetic to such an approach, many are more comfortable and familiar with lecture and recitation situations and tend to stress right answers over hypothesis generation, prediction, data collection, and analysis. Moreover, to benefit from project-based instruction, students need to have considerable skill in using learning, problem-solving, and metacognitive strategies. Thus, scaffolding is especially critical for students who are not proficient in using thinking strategies. Teachers themselves need models and support in leaning how to help students learn.

Assessment

Project-based instruction requires that teachers be able to ascertain what students know about the problem before beginning the project, their level of understanding during execution of the project, and what they learn as a result. The typical standardized test or work-book question focuses primarily on low-level comprehension and is inappropriate for examining short- and long-term benefits of project-based instruction. Examples of informal measures that can provide guidance and feedback for both teachers and students are journal or notebook entries, portfolio assessment, clinical interviews, and examining student discourse. However, teachers need help in using such techniques to diagnose student understanding because they are less structured, more clinical, and more time consuming.

Management

Project-based instruction engages children in high-level and com-plex learning activities that often have no right answer or one way to be accomplished. This type of academic work is difficult for teachers to manage and sustain (Blumenfeld et al., 1987; Doyle, 1983, 1986; Stake & Easley, 1978; Tobin & Capie, 1988). High-level cognitive tasks are associated with lower completion and higher error rates; these factors slow the momentum of a lesson, increase student need for help, and heighten the potential for disorder. As a result, teachers often feel pressured to simplify material or suspend accountability for learning under these circumstances (Doyle, Sanford, Clements, French, & Emmer, 1983). If teachers capitulate to these pressures when using project-based instruction, many of the putative motiva-tional and learning benefits will not materialize.

Classroom environment

Project-based instruction relies on a classroom climate that pro-motes inquiry and a mastery of orientation. However, many class-rooms promote performance rather than a mastery orientation to learning. Teachers in the former type of classrooms stress correct answers, grades, competition, and public comparison with others (Ames & Archer, 1988). Consequently, students are less likely to take risks, worry more about errors, and make less use of cognitive and metacognitive learning strategies to obtain greater understanding.

THE ROLE OF TECHNOLOGY

Technology can play a powerful role in enhancing student and teacher motivation to do projects and in helping students and teach-ers implement projects. In this section we describe how technology can contribute to student motivation to do projects by enhancing interest and, more important, supporting learning and the production of artifacts by making information accessible. The aim is to show how technology can share some of the teacher's responsibility for helping students as they engage in project-based learning. We also describe how technology can help inform teachers about project-based learning and aid in project implementation. Finally, in recognition that technology, like all educational innovations, is not without its problems, we raise issues for future research.

> Technology can contribute to how interesting and valuable students find projects.

Technology and Students
Enhancing interest
Technology can contribute to how interesting and valuable students find projects. Students are more likely to take part in project-based learning when projects focus on questions that they perceive as valuable, are challenging, include a variety or activities, are realistic, allow interaction with others, and result in authentic products. Technology can enhance challenge, variety, and choice by providing multiple levels of tasks to match student knowledge and proficiency, access to numerous sources of information that allow breadth in project questions, and offer many possibilities for artifact production. Moreover, tasks may be perceived as more authentic by students because the computer can access real data, can expand interaction and collaboration with others via networks, and emulate tool use by experts to produce artifacts.

Although there certainly are individual differences in its appeal, observational research (Cognition and Technology Group, 1990) suggests that technology can make a project more interesting. In studying the Geometry Tutor, Kafai (1989) observed that students preferred computer-based over noncomputer-based geometry instruction and asked for additional problems to solve using the Proof Tutor. Similarly, Scardamalia, Bereiter, McLean, Swallow, and Woodruff (1989) showed how student control of learning and immediacy of feedback influenced student motivation to work on difficult tasks with computers. Moreover, Malone and Lepper (1987) found that computer activities motivated students because they allowed for control, were interactive, provided immediate results, and allowed for different levels of challenge.

Access to information

In the process of doing projects, students need access to information about key ideas, concepts, and subject matter topics that might arise. Technology makes information more accessible. Traditionally, teachers and books have been key sources of information. Consulting other sources such as archives or references like the *Reader's Guide to Periodical Literature* is, at minimum, time consuming and sometimes is not possible, depending on the student's geographical location or available resources. Electronic data bases allow learners access to massive amounts of information that are easily obtainable while sitting at a personal computer. The information can be either static, such as electronic encyclopedias or historical records, or live, such as transmissions from weather satellites. Similarly, networks and various forms of teleconferencing "expand the classroom walls," providing access to peers and experts in other locations. For example, the National Geographic Society's KidsNet network (Tinker & Papert, 1989) provides the opportunity for upper elementary students to gather local data on the pH of rain water. Through the use of networks, students discuss their findings with scientists and share results with those collected by students in other locations.

> Through the use of networks, students discuss their findings with scientists and share results with those collected by students in other locations.

Obviously, simply providing access to information does not guarantee that it will be useful to the students. A central issue is how to design and organize these information sources to be profitable to students. Progress is being made on ways to structure information systems to be more useful to students working on authentic tasks. For example, Scardamalia and Bereiter (1991) studied methods to structure computer-based discussions of writing among peers, such as providing prompts and starting sentences for critiques.

Active representation

The multimodal and multimedia capabilities of technology not only enhance the physical accessibility of the information, but also facilitate its intellectual accessibility. In addition to text, there has been an explosive growth in the use of media—sound, graphs, color pictures, and even video—on the computer. This variety provides for representation of single concepts in multiple, simultaneous modalities. These multiple representations can enhance student understanding. For example, Kozna, Russell, Johnston, and Dershimer (1991) explored representation of chemistry concepts via video, animation, and textual mathematics equations simultaneously on a single screen.

Technology also allows students to manipulate and construct their own representations easily and to do so in several media. Harel and Papert (1990) noted significant increases in mathematics learning among their students who devised various graphical and textual representations of fractions using Logo programs. Simulations and microworlds, such as those developed by diSessa (1982) and White and Horwitz (1987), allow students to explore and manipulate ideas actively in artificial environments that minimize extraneous detail and make it easier to note interactions between the available variables. Similarly, microcomputer-based laboratories (MBL) allow students to collect real-time data: Students can ask "what if" questions, use electronic sensors to test their predictions, and view the results of these experiments in various forms like graphs or charts (Friedler, Nachmias, & Linn, 1990; Linn, Songer, Lewis, & Stern, 1991; Mokros & Tinker, 1987). Finally, some data base systems provide facilities for students to organize and create their own indices; the process of navigating through and organizing the information can help students to create their own mental representations of that information.

Because technology allows students to explore, construct, and easily alter representations, as well as control the process, motivation is likely to be affected positively. Computers respond quickly, and the cost of change is relatively minimal. Once students are familiar with software applications and the power and versatility that they provide, they may be more willing to explore alternatives actively and take more risks. Thus, the motivational qualities of computers as cognitive tools are likely to be enhanced when software has been well learned and its use is relatively automatic. When students have developed competence with software, mental effort can be devoted to the intellectual task of creating artifacts, not to the details of production. Consequently, students' engagement can be more "mindful" (Salomon, Perkins, & Globerson, 1991), and the potential of project-based leaning can be realized.

Structuring the process: Providing tactical and strategic support
The opportunity to view, manipulate, and create multiple representations using technology does not ensure that students will take
advantage of these capabilities in a manner
that enhances understanding. Students need

Technology also can
be designed to pro-
vide strategic support
by specifying and
explaining steps the
learner should follow.

to use cognitive and metacognitive strategies
as they gather, manipulate, and integrate
information and as they work though the
phases of a project—setting goals, planning,
monitoring and evaluating progress, and producing and revising artifacts. Although the
teacher serves a critical role in guiding students and modeling learning processes,
a focus of considerable study is how to design the technology itself to
promote what Salomon and Globerson (1987) termed "mindfulness."

Whereas early applications of technology emphasized specific
skill acquisition, as in computer-assisted instruction (Suppes, 1980),
more recent applications emphasize the learning process. Technology can be designed to provide tactical and strategic support. Tactical support can be provided by prompts that suggest the learner use
a particular operation or ask for articulations or explanations. For
example, Linn et al. (1991) used prompts in an MBL environment to
encourage students to make predictions after the experiment. These
prompts can serve as cognitive aids in learning. At a macro level,
software can be designed to offer both strategic and tactical support.
Such programs guide the learner to be systematic and to use coherent routes in problem solving. The intent is to place students on a
trajectory toward gaining an expertlike process. For example,
Soloway (1991a) developed the Goal/PlanCode Editor, which structures the process of writing PASCAL programs. To encourage greater
expertise in students' processes, the software requires students to
decompose problems into pieces and to articulate goals for a piece
before writing a code.

Technology also can be designed to provide strategic support
by specifying and explaining steps the learner should follow. For
instance, CSILE (Computer-Supported Intentional Learning Environments), a program for supporting text composition, provides
icons that suggest stages of process development such as indicating
cognitive goals, plans for pursuing them, and target dates
(Scardamalia et al., 1989; Hawkins & Pea, 1987) structures the

process of developing research questions by providing both explicit process representation and detail-level prompting.

Another strength of technology is that levels of tactical and strategic support can be graduated to accommodate differences among individuals in knowledge of content and process necessary for projects. Supports also can accommodate individual change as a student's knowledge of the content and process develops across time. Soloway (1991a) examined how to design software in order to fade scaffolds. In a related vein, they also have experimented with approaches that allow learners themselves to alter the degree of scaffolding.

Diagnosing and correcting errors
Because of the complexity of project-based learning, errors can be made over a wide range of processes and content. Indeed, errors and false starts are an inherent part of doing projects. Students need to evaluate thinking about the problem, their solution, and their products. That is, they need to diagnose and correct errors in specific parts of the project, in the process that was followed, or on the artifacts produced. Technological support for locating errors can be provided directly via explicit statements of where errors occurred and how to correct them or more indirectly by guiding the students' review with suggestions that vary in specificity (e.g., J. R. Anderson, Boyle, & Reiser, 1985). Moreover, programs like INQUIRE that provide explicit support for reflection on the process can indirectly help students identify difficulties in the steps they followed.

Although making errors is an inevitable part of project-based learning, the cost is not the same for all types of errors. When students make errors on tactical components of project work, it is likely that technology can help convert the error from an indicator of inability to a sign of progress toward successful construction of artifacts. Once tactical errors are diagnosed, technology makes change easy. Because the cost of change is cheap, students can explore alternative solutions without undue expense. For example, Nachmias and Linn (1987) found that students learning to interpret graphs through MBL equipment recognized inaccurate or flawed graphs more easily than did students who did not learn with technological support. They suggested that students who used MBL equipment were able to generate graphs more quickly and thus were able to explore a range of both good and bad graphical representations.

Not all errors, however, are easy to change. Rectifying fundamental strategic errors might involve considerably more cost to the student. For example, students who have invested considerable time and energy to produce an MBL representation of an artifact might have considerable difficulty interpreting errors as cheap. Such work might entail significant amounts of time and cognitive work to search data bases, videodisks, and text in order to construct an artifact. If the wrong data bases were selected, or if visuals on a videodisk were inaccurate representations of concepts and principles, then students might be far less willing to revise material in order to improve the quality of final artifacts. The issue might have considerable impact on students' motivation to sustain work on projects.

> As already mentioned, artifacts are significant as externalizations of the student's understanding . . .

Managing complexity and aiding production
Students who are working on projects produce a range of intermediate and final artifacts. As already mentioned, artifacts are significant as externalizations of the student's understanding because they can be shared and critiqued. The computer can help students generate artifacts by minimizing physical and mental detail. Application software such as word processors, spreadsheets, desktop publishing programs, and drawing programs automate the generation of attractive illustrations and meaningful graphs and compute complex series of equations. New programs being developed (Guzdial & Soloway, 1991; Pea, Boyle, & de Vogel, 1990; Soloway, 1991b) allow students to manipulate video, text, graphics, and animations to develop multimedia compositions and presentations. Automation of the details of production frees the student to explore greater levels of complexity in the content of the project and the design of artifacts. Obviously, however, if using the application is complicated or too demanding, the student is less likely to invest the time in mastering the tool and thus will not benefit from its possibilities.

Summary
Technology affords considerable potential for motivating students to carry out projects. We have detailed ways in which it can contribute both directly by increasing students' interest and value and indirectly

by aiding the teacher in supporting students as they gather information relevant to project questions and use that information to generate artifacts that represent their understanding. How technology can best be designed to serve these functions remains to be determined. Many questions remain: How much support should be provided? Is there a danger of "de-skilling" students because they rely heavily on the technology? How can supports be built into a program to be used by a range of students, from the complete novice to the relative expert? How do we ensure that students use these supports, and continue to use them? How do we make error correction easy, but still thoughtful? How can the experiences on the computer be structured so that learning is transferred (Salomon et al., 1991)? It is important to note that, for the most part, these questions are not unique to technology but apply to traditional instruction as well.

A critical issue, we believe, is that technology supplements but cannot supplant the teacher in helping students do projects. Moreover, its contribution depends considerably on the culture and norms the teacher creates, within which technology is used and whether it is employed as an integral tool in project execution. Therefore, a key research issue is how to promote this interplay between teacher and technology in facilitating projects and to determine what roles are appropriate for technology. Other concerns are how to help teachers use the technology to learn about and implement projects and help them exploit technology's benefits for students. We consider these issues next.

Technology and Teachers

We have described possibilities for how technology can share some of the teacher's role in sustaining student motivation in project-based learning. Instituting project-based learning can be rewarding for teachers; however, because of the new and unfamiliar demands it creates, it can also be problematic. The implementation of project-based learning is a complex and multifaceted endeavor. There is likely to be a considerable gap between existing practices and practices called for in project-based education. Technology can play a role in supporting teachers as they learn about and implement projects in the classroom. Specifically, teachers need to know about (a) project content and powerful ways to illustrate that content, (b) project-based instruction (e.g., how to help students plan, carry out, and evaluate their work), (c) management of project-based learning, and (d) adaptation or generation of projects in light of their students' specific needs.

Research on teaching and teacher development suggests how technological material can support teachers as they think about and cope with the problems they are likely to face in doing projects. These approaches (for a review, see Clark & Peterson, 1986) view teaching as highly complex cognitive activity, in which diverse sources of knowledge must be integrated. These perspectives focus on the teacher as a reflective professional (Schon, 1983), in contrast to the previous emphasis on skills and techniques. Key elements in these approaches are the teacher's thinking, decision making, planning, and reflection. Essentially, the view is that teaching involves learning; like their students, teachers construct their knowledge of subject content, pedagogical content, curriculum, and students and draw on this knowledge in designing instruction (Shulman, 1986, 1987). Project support materials should not only enhance the teacher's knowledge base about projects but also aid in the planning process. In addition, the materials should not be prescriptive. Instead, they should focus on ways to help teachers create a set of experiences by adapting existing projects or generating new ones in light of their particular teaching circumstances and students. The materials should allow teachers to access information about projects in a variety of ways.

To address such needs, we are building a Project Support Environment (PSE) for teachers that provides information about these areas. In particular, the PSE will be a hypermedia information system that will enable teachers to see actual videotapes of implementation of project-based learning on the computer; it will enable them to access information about content and instructional issues from a concrete (e.g., how to help students make predictions) and more theoretical perspective (what factors promote thoughtfulness). It includes a tool that allows teachers to construct plans and networking capabilities to facilitate communications among teachers. Because the PSE is a constructive tool, it provides access to information from many different points. In following sections, we briefly describe how a system like the one we envision can contribute to teachers' implementation of project-based learning.

Content and pedagogical content knowledge
Like their students, teachers can benefit from the information access, multiple representation, multimedia, and knowledge capabilities of technology. Via networks, teachers can get information about the central ideas and concepts in projects as well as the numerous incidental questions that are likely to arise. Their understanding is likely to be both broadened and depended because they can see information represented in a variety of ways and also use the technology to manipulate and create

> Technology can also help improve teachers' pedagogical content knowledge.

their own representations. For example, Krajcik, Layman, Starr, and Magnusson (1991) used technology to enhance teachers' knowledge of temperature and heat energy concepts.

Technology can also help improve teachers' pedagogical content knowledge. Methods of helping students understand ideas or concepts (which activities, explanations, and analogies teachers have tried that worked or did not work) as well as information about possible student misconceptions or alternative conceptions can be stored in a hypermedia system, illustrated visually, and shared among teachers through networks. For instance, instructional examples might be shown to teachers who ask, "How can I explain motivation?" Currently, teachers are limited to suggestions in manuals, their own experiences, or conversations with colleagues. Technology offers an exciting opportunity for vastly expanding the sources of teachers' information.

Instruction
Hypermedia information systems that combine text, video, animation, graphics, and audio can be developed in which teachers can see examples of how others have implemented projects. For instance, teachers can ask questions about how to encourage metacognition ("How can I help students generate and test predictions?"), about events ("How can I introduce projects?"), or about technology ("How can I use MBL to help students do what-if experiences?") and see video examples of how other teachers dealt with these questions. In addition, video clips can be annotated by the teachers pictured to include information regarding what they had intended to do and their reflections on what worked and what they would do differently the next time.

Planning and managing

Teachers will need to tailor existing projects or develop new projects to meet the specific needs and constraints of their classroom, school, and community. Also, they will need to develop plans for designing and implementing projects in their specific contexts. Technology can provide support for planning such design activity and for carrying out those plans. Moreover, these plans themselves are artifacts that can be shared with and critiqued by others and reflected on and revised by the teacher.

As part of the PSE, we have implemented and tested in the classroom a first version of such project-planning software, called IByD (Instruction By Design) with preservice teachers. The program is an expert shell that provides preservice teachers with strategic support for processes (developing goals, selecting activities, identifying evaluations, and describing possible instructional examples) and tactical support by requiring the user to provide rationales for choices and to show the plan's coherence by visually illustrating and explaining how elements of the plan are linked. Preliminary results (Blumenfeld, Soloway, Urdan, & Brade, 1991) suggest that IByD helped structure the process of planning so that rationales of plans generated by computer users were significantly more systematic and explicit than those of the plans produced by noncomputer-using subjects in the same teacher education course.

> ... technology can directly support teachers as they learn about and implement projects ...

Summary

The technology teachers need to support their efforts at realizing effective project-based instruction corresponds to the technological tools that professionals in other areas routinely use (e.g., planning software, telecommunications software, and multimedia data bases). Although there is less consensus regarding whether teachers need such tools, few would argue against technological support for teachers that is commensurate with technological support in the commercial sector. We have argued that technology can directly support teachers as they learn about and implement projects and as they support student learning.

CONCLUSION

We have argued in this article that there is considerable promise in the notion of project-based education to enhance motivation and thought as students attempt to learn in classrooms. We have indicated factors in project design that are likely to affect motivation and thought, examined how teacher implementation of projects can influence motivation and thought, and described how technology can support students and teachers as they work on projects so that motivation and thought are sustained. Our main interest has been to examine motivational and instructional issues that need to be incorporated in attempts to research and implement project-based learning.

Projects in which students pursue long-term investigations of a significant question and produce artifacts that represent answers to those questions have the potential to motivate students and help them better understand subject matter content. The idea of project-based learning certainly is not new; however, considerable advances in our knowledge about motivation, learning, teachers, and classrooms increase the possibility of success now. Although there obviously will be individual differences in student reactions, projects can be designed to include elements that are likely to enhance most students' interest and value, including variety, challenge, choice, cooperation, and closure in the service of answering real questions. In addition, by considering students' prior knowledge and thinking skills, projects can be designed to support students so that they feel able to succeed.

Although research and theory have provided answers to many important questions related to implementing project-based education, we need to know a great deal more about how to sustain student motivation and thought in projects. Project-based learning requires considerable knowledge, effort, persistence, and self-regulation on the part of students; they need to device plans, gather information, evaluate both the findings and their approach, and generate and revise artifacts. Such requirements are not easily met. Teachers will play a critical role in helping students in this process, by shaping opportunities for learning, guiding students' thinking, and helping them construct new understandings. However, project-based learning is likely to pose difficulties for teachers too. They may need help with content, with new instructional forms, and with implementation and management of projects.

We argue that technology can make substantial contributions to ameliorating these problems associated with project learning. It can enhance student interest because it can contribute to variety, challenge, interaction with others, and generation of artifacts. Technology can aid the teacher in achieving goals of project-based learning by making information more physically and intellectually accessible, guiding and promoting the use of learning strategies, and aiding in the production of artifacts. Moreover, it can support the teacher in learning about and successfully implementing projects. Although many questions remain about how to design and use technology effectively for these purposes, the fact that technology is becoming more powerful, available, and affordable makes determining how to utilize its power to motivate project-based learning in classrooms a timely and important endeavor for those seeking to improve education.

It is important to emphasize that project design, teaching, and use of technology all need to be considered as opportunities for marshalling existing student motivation, creating opportunities for motivation, and sustaining motivation once project-based learning activities are underway. Furthermore, we have argued that motivation and cognitive engagement are interative—one or the other becomes more or less salient during the course of project work. We have suggested potential questions that might help shape an agenda for research on learning and motivation in project-based education. Answers to such questions are likely to help guide the most recent wave of curriculum reform as educators address the problems that their predecessors faced and failed to solve.

Acknowledgments: We thank Jere Brophy and Paul Pintrich for their demanding and insightful comments on earlier drafts of this article.

NOTES

1. We use the term artifacts to *denote* sharable and critiquable externalization of students' cognitive work in classrooms. In contrast to the use of the word in other fields, our use of the term is synonymous with *product*. However, we use *artifact* to denote that the results of student's cognitive work proceed through intermediate phases and are continuously subject to revision and improvement.

REFERENCES

Ames, C., & Archer, J. (1988). Achievement goals in the classroom: Students' learning strategies and motivation processes. *Journal of Educational Psychology, 80,* 260–267.

Anderson, C. W., & Roth, J. K. (1989). Teaching for meaningful and self-regulated learning of science. In. J. Brophy (Ed.), *Teaching for meaningful understanding and self-regulated learning* (pp. 265–309). Greenwich, CT: JAI.

Anderson, C. W., & Smith, E. (1987). Teaching science. In V. Koehler (Ed.), *Educator's handbook: A research perspective* (pp. 84–11). New York: Longman.

Anderson, J., Boyle, C., & Reiser, B. (1985). Intelligent tutoring systems. *Science, 228,* 456–462.

Anderson, L. (1989). Classroom instruction. In M. Reynolds (Ed.), *Knowledge base of the beginning teacher* (pp. 101–115). New York: American Association of Colleges for Teacher Education/Pergamon.

Bennett, N., DesForges, C., Cockburn, A., & Wilkinson, B. (1984). *The quality of pupil learning experiences.* Hillsdale, NJ: Lawrence Erlbaum Associates, Inc.

Blumenfeld, P. C. (in press). The task and the teacher: Enhancing student thoughtfulness in science. In. J. Brophy (Eds.), *Advances in research on teaching: Planning and managing learning tasks and activities* (Vol. 3). Greenwich, CT: JAI.

Blumenfeld, P., & Meece, J. (1988). Task factors, teacher behavior and students' involvement and use of learning strategies in science. *Elementary School Journal, 88,* 235–250.

Blumenfeld, P. C., Mergendoller, J., & Swarthout, D. (1987). Task as a heuristic for understanding student learning and motivation. *Journal of Curriculum Studies, 19,* 135–148.

Blumenfeld, P. C., Puro, P., & Mergendoller, J. (in press). Translating motivation into thoughtfulness. In H. Marshall (Ed.), *Supporting student learning: Roots of educational restructuring.* Norwood, NJ: Ablex.

Blumenfeld, P. C., Soloway, E., Urdan, T., & Brade, K. (1991, July). *Designing instruction: Improving planning of pre-service teachers.* Paper presented at the NATO (North Atlantic Treaty Organization) Workshop on Computers and Instruction, Amsterdam.

Bossert. (1989). Cooperative activities in classrooms. In E. Rothkoph (Ed.), *Review of research in education* (pp. 225–250). Washington, DC: American Educational Research Association.

Bredderman, T. (1983). Effects of activity-based elementary science on student outcomes: A quantitative synthesis. *Review of Educational Research, 53,* 499–518.

Brophy, J. (1983). Conceptualizing student motivation. *Educational Psychologist, 18,* 200–215.

————. (1989). Advances in research on teaching: *Teaching for understanding (Vol. 1).* Greenwich, CT: JAI.

Brophy, J., & Alleman, (1991). Activities as instructional tools: A framework for instructional analysis and evaluation. *Educational Researcher, 20,* 9–23.

Brown, J. S., Collins, A., & Duguid, P. (1989). Situated cognition of learning. *Educational Researcher, 18,* 32–42.

Brunner, C., Hawkins, J., Mann, F., & Moller, B. (1990). Designing INQUIRE. In B. Bowen (Ed.), *Design for learning: Research-based design of technology for learning* (pp. 27–34). Cupertino, CA: Apple Computer Company.

Clark, C. M., & Peterson, P. L. (1986). Teachers' thought processes. In M. Wittrock (Ed.), *Handbook of research on teaching* (3rd ed., pp. 255–296). New York: Macmillan.

Cognition and Technology Group. (1990). Anchored instruction and its relationship to situated cognition. *Educational Researcher, 19,* 2–10.

Confrey, J. (1990). A review of the research on student conceptions in mathematics, science, and programming. In C. B. Cazden (Ed.), *Review of research in education* (pp. 3–56). Washington DC: American Educational Research Association.

Cohen, E. (1986). *Designing groupwork.* New York: Teacher College Press.

Corno, L., & Mandinach, E. (1983). The role of cognitive engagement in classroom learning and motivation. *Educational Psychologist, 18,* 88–108.

Corno, L., & Rohrkemper, M. (1985). The intrinsic motivation to learn in classrooms. In C. Ames & R. Ames (Eds.)*; Research on motivation in education: The classroom milieu* (Vol. 2, pp. 53–84). New York: Academic.

Deci, E. L., & Ryan, R. M. (1987). The support of autonomy and the control of behavior. *Journal of Personality and Social Psychology, 53,* 1024–1037.

diSessa, A. (1982). Unlearning Aristotelian physics: A study of knowledge-based learning. *Cognitive Science, 6,* 37–75.

Doyle, W. (1983). Academic work. *Review of Educational Research, 53,* 159–200.

————. (1986). Classroom organization and management. In M. Wittrock (Ed.), *Handbook of research on teaching* (pp. 392–431). New York: Macmillian.

Doyle, W., Sanford, J., Clements, B., French, B., & Emmer, E. (1983). *Managing academic tasks. An interim report of the junior high school study* (Research and Development Rep. No. 6186). Austin: University of Texas, Research and Development Center for Teacher Education.

Driver, R., & Oldham, V. (1986). A constructionist approach to curriculum development in science. *Studies in Science Education, 13,* 105–122.

Dweck, C. S., & Elliot, E. S. (1983). Achievement motivation. In P. Mussen (Ed.), *Handbook of child psychology* (pp. 643–691). New York: Wiley.

Eichinger, D. C., Anderson, C. W., Palincsar, A. S., & David, Y. M. (1991, April). *An illustration of the roles of content knowledge, scientific argument, and social norms in collaborative problem solving.* Paper presented at the meeting of the American Educational Research Association, Chicago.

Friedler, Y., Nachmias, R., & Linn, M. (1990). Learning scientific skills in microcomputer-based laboratory. *Journal of Research in Science Teaching, 27,* 173–189.

Good, T., McCaslin, M., & Reyes, B. (in press). Investigating workgroups to promote problem solving in mathematics. In J. Brophy (Ed.), *Advances in research on teaching: Planning and managing learning tasks and activities* (Vol. 3). Greenwich, CT: JAI Press.

Goodlad, J. (1983). *A place called school.* New York: McGraw-Hill.

Guzdial, M., & Soloway, E. (1991, July). *MediaText: Design rationale and classroom experiences.* Presented at the Workshop on Intelligent MultiMedia Interfaces, Anaheim, CA.

Harel, I., & Papert, S. (1990). Software design as a learning environment. *Interactive Learning Environments, 1,* 1–32.

Harter, S. (1983). Developmental perspectives on the self system. In P. Mussen (Ed.), *A Handbook of child psychology* (Vol. 4, pp. 275–386). New York: Wiley.

Hawkins, J., & Pea, R. D. (1987). Tools for bridging the cultures of everyday and scientific thinking. *Journal for Research on Science Teaching, 24,* 291–307.

Hofstein, A., & Lunetta, V. (1982). The role of the laboratory in science teaching: Neglected aspects of research. *Review of Educational Research, 52,* 201–217.

Kafai, Y. (1989). What happens if you introduce an intelligent tutoring system in the classroom: A case study of the Geometry Tutor. In *Proceedings of the National Educational Computing Conference* (pp. 46–57). Eugene, OR: University of Oregon, International Society of Technology in Education.

Kozma, R. B., Russell, J., Johnston, J., & Dershimer, C. (1991). *College students understanding of chemical equilibrium.* Unpublished manuscript, University of Michigan, National Center for Research and Improvement of Post-Secondary Teaching and Learning, Ann Arbor.

Krajcik, J. S., & Layman, J. W. (1989, April). *Middle school teachers' conceptions of heat and temperature: Personal and teaching knowledge.* Paper presented at the annual meeting of the National Association for Research in Science Teaching, San Francisco.

Krajcik, J. S., Layman, J. W., Starr, M. L., & Magnusson, S. (1991, April). *The development middle school teachers' content knowledge and pedagogical content knowledge of heat energy and temperature.* Paper presented at the annual meeting of the American Educational Research Association, Chicago.

Lepper, M. R. (1988). Motivational considerations in the study of instruction. *Cognition and Instruction, 5,* 289–309.

Lewis, E. L., & Linn, M. C. (1989, April). *Heat energy and temperature concepts of adolescents and experts: Implications for curricular improvement.* Paper presented at the annual meeting of the National Association for Research in Science Teaching, San Francisco.

Linn, M., Songer, N. B., Lewis, E. L., & Stern, J. (1991). Using technology to teach thermodynamics: Achieving integrated understanding. In D. L. Ferguson (Ed.), *Advanced technologies in the teaching of mathematics and science.* Berlin: Springer-Verlag.

Malone, T. W., & Lepper, M. R. (1987). Making learning fun: A taxonomy of intrinsic motivations for learning. In R. Snow & M. Farr (Eds.), *Aptitude, learning, and instruction: Conative and affective process analyses* (Vol. 3, pp. 223–253). Hillsdale, NJ: Lawrence Erlbaum Associates, Inc.

Marx, R. W., & Walsh, J. (1988). Learning from academic tasks. *Elementary School Journal, 88,* 207–220.

Meece, J. L., Blumenfeld, P. C., & Hoyle, R. H. (1988). Students' goal orientation and cognitive engagement in classroom activities. *Journal of Educational Psychology, 80,* 514–523.

Meece, J. L., Blumenfeld, P. C., & Puro, P. (1989). A motivational analysis of elementary science learning environments. In M. Matyas, K. Tobin, & B. Fraser (Eds.), *Looking into windows: Qualitative research in science education* (pp. 13–23). Washington, DC: American Association for the Advancement of Science.

Mokros, J. R., & Tinker, R. F. (1987). The impact of microcomputer-based labs on children's ability to interpret graphs. *Journal of Research in Science Teaching, 24,* 369–383.

Nachmias, R., & Linn, M. C. (1987). Evaluations of science laboratory data: The role of computer-presented information. *Journal of Research in Science Teaching, 24,* 491–506.

Nicholls, J. G., Pataschnick, M., & Nolen, S. (1985). Adolescents' theories of education. *Journal of Educational Psychology, 77,* 683–692.

Nolen, S. B. (1988). Reasons for studying: Motivational orientations and study strategies. *Cognition and Instruction, 5,* 269–287.

Nussbaum, J., & Novick, S. (1982). Alternative frameworks, conceptual conflict and accommodation: Toward a principled teaching strategy. *Instructional Science, 11,* 183–200.

Osborne, R., & Freyberg, P. (1985). *Learning in science: The implications of children's science.* London: Heinemann.

Paris, S. G., Lipson, M. Y., & Wixson, K. K. (1983). Becoming a strategic reader. *Contemporary Educational Psychology, 8,* 293–316.

Pea, R. D., Boyle, E., & de Vogel, R. (1990). Design spaces for multimedia composition. In B. Bowen (Ed.), *Design for learning* (pp. 37–41). Cupertino, CA: Apple Computer Company.

Pintrich, P. R., & De Groot, E. W. (1990). Motivational and self-regulated learning components of classroom academic. *Journal of Educational Psychology, 82,* 33–40.

Pokay, P., & Blumenfeld, P. C. (1990). Predicting achievement early and late in the semester: The role of motivation and use of learning strategies. *Journal of Educational Psychology, 82,* 41–50.

Resnick, L. B. (1987). Learning in school and out. *Educational Researcher, 16,* 13–20.

Rohrkemper, M., & Corno, L. (1988). Success and failure on classroom tasks: Adaptive learning and classroom teaching. *Elementary School Journal, 88,* 297–312.

Rosenshine, B. V. (1987). Explicit teaching. In D. C. Berliner & B. Rosenshine (Eds.), *Talks to teachers* (pp. 75–92). New York: Lane Akers.

Rosenshine, B., & Stevens, R. (1986). Teaching functions. In M. C. Wittrock (Ed.), *Handbook of research on teaching* (3rd ed., pp. 376–391). New York: Macmillan.

Salomon, G. (1983). The differential investment of mental effort in learning from different sources. *Educational Psychologist, 18,* 42–50.

Salomon, G., & Globerson, T. (1987). Skill may not be enough: The role of mindfulness in learning and transfer. *International Journal of Educational Research, 11,* 623–638.

Salomon, G., Perkins, D., & Globerson, T. (1991). Partners in cognition: Extending human intelligence with intelligent technologies. *Educational Researcher, 20,* 2–9.

Scardamalia, M., & Bereiter, C. (1991). Higher levels of agency for children in knowledge building: A challenge for the design of new knowledge of media. *Journal of the Learning Sciences, 1,* 37–68.

Scardamalia, M., & Bereiter, C., McLean, R., Swallow, J., & Woodruff, E. (1989). Computer-supported intentional learning environments. *Journal of Educational Computing Research, 5,* 51–68.

Schön, D. (1983). *The reflective practitioner.* New York: Basic.

Shavelson, R., & Stern, P. (1981). Research on teachers' pedagogical thoughts, judgments, decisions, and behavior. *Review of Educational Research, 51,* 455–498.

Shulman, L. (1986). Paradigms and research programs in the study of teaching: A contemporary perspective. In M. Wittrock (Ed.), *Handbook of research on teaching* (3rd ed., pp. 3–36). New York: Macmillan.

Shulman, L. S. (1987). Knowledge and teaching. *Harvard Educational Review, 56,* 1–22.

Sizer, T. (1984). *Horace's compromise: The dilemma of the American high school.* Boston: Houghton-Mifflin.

Slavin, R. E. (1983). *Cooperative learning.* New York: Longman.

Smith, C., & Neale, D. C. (1989). The construction of subject matter knowledge in primary science teaching. *Teaching and Teacher Education, 5,* 1–20.

Soloway, E. (1991a). Design's the name . . . Technology's the game. In B. Bowen (Ed.), *Accelerating innovation* (pp. 71–78). Cupertino, CA: Apple Computer Company.

———. (1991b, June). *Mediatext: The Brownie instamatic of multi-media.* Paper presented at the National Educational Computing Conference, Phoenix.

Stake, R. E., & Easley, J. A. (1978). *Case studies in science education* (Vol. 2). Washington, DC: U.S. Government Printing Office (No. 038-000-0037603).

Suppes, P. (1980). Computer-based mathematics instruction. In R. P. Taylor (Ed.), *The computer in the school: Tutor, tool, tutee* (pp. 215–230). New York: Teachers College Press.

Tinker, R. F., & Papert, S. (1989). Tools for science education. In J. Ellis (Ed.), *1988 AETS yearbook: Information technology and science education.* Columbus, OH: ERIC Clearinghouse for Science, Mathematics, and Environmental Education.

Tobin, K., & Capie, W. (1988). Active teaching for higher cognitive learning in science. *International Journal of Science Education, 10,* 17–27.

Toulmin, S. E. (1972). *Human understanding.* Princeton, NJ: Princeton University Press.

Webb, N. (1982). Student interaction and learning in small groups. *Review of Educational Research, 52,* 421–445.

Weinstein, C., & Mayer, R. (1986). The teaching of learning strategies. In M. Wittrock (Ed.), *Handbook of research on teaching* (pp. 315–327). New York: Macmillan.

White, B. Y., & Horwitz, P. (1987). *Thinker Tools: Enabling children to understand physical laws* (BBN Report No. 8470). Cambridge, MA: Bolt Beranek, & Newman.

Winne, P. H., & Marx, R. W. (1982). Students' and teachers' views of thinking processes for classroom learning. *Elementary School Journal, 82,* 493–518.

————. (1987). The best tools teachers have—their students' thinking. In D. C. Berliner & B. Rosenshine (Eds.), *Talks to teachers* (pp. 267–304). New York: Lane Akers.

————. (1989). A cognitive-processing analysis of motivation with classroom tasks. In C. Ames & R. Ames (Eds.), *Research on motivation in education* (Vol. 3, pp. 223–257). New York: Academic.

Wittrock, M. (1986). Students' thought processes. In M. Wittrock (Ed.), *Handbook of research on teaching* (pp. 297–327). New York: Macmillan.

Section 4

Innovations . . . Problem-Based Learning

A problem well stated is a problem half-solved.

—Charles F. Kettering

In addition to the previous section featuring classroom applications, this grouping highlights articles about special applications. These include discussions on problem-based learning (PBL) in the interdisciplinary classroom, in gifted programs, for those who are not college-bound, and for instructional leaders in educational administration programs. For each of these applications, specific circumstances are cited; yet, together they demonstrate the generic appeal of the PBL method.

Stepien, Gallagher, and Workman present information about the use of PBL in both traditional, discipline-based classrooms and in interdisciplinary approaches at the high school level for gifted education students. In a science setting, they examine modern dilemmas resulting from the advances in science technology, while in the American studies class they use the post-holing technique for depth of understanding on particular areas of study within the unit. In both, the PBL investigative strategies are discussed (problem definition, information gathering, log exercises, resolutions).

In another gifted education application, Pearson begins with the idea that "it's a messy job, but somebody's got to do it" as a segway into a discussion of the hands-on nature of PBL. Learning with PBL is as "messy" and unpredictable as the messy situations in the real world. The author believes that it is possible to simulate the conditions of trial and error, flexible thinking to the teamwork in the classroom, and, in this case, in the gifted classroom. Both long-term projects and short problem-solving experiments are highlighted. This discussion, as in others, emphasizes the role of the teacher in asking key questions and taking on the guise of a coach, rather than a giver of knowledge.

In contrast to innovative applications with the gifted, the third article in this section stresses the appropriateness of PBL in a comprehensive math class. Building on the premise that most students are capable of thinking about mathematics and complex concepts, the curriculum is designed to meet college entrance requirements and to prepare youngsters to use problem-solving skills on the job. Students deal with problems about maximizing the profits of a baker and delve into intriguing units entitled Meadows or Malls?, Shadows, and Do Bees Build It Best? Combining traditional math with the PBL approach, write these authors, has yielded positive results for students.

As in each of the previous sections, the selections stand alone and the reader may choose among the titles, but together, read as a unit, they seem to stretch the imagination about the possibilities about PBL as a curricular/instructional approach across a spectrum of learning situations.

Problem-Based Learning for Traditional and Interdisciplinary Classrooms

by William J. Stepien, Shelagh A. Gallagher, & David Workman

Classroom instruction in problem solving often takes the form of presenting neat, verification-style problems to students at the end of a period of learning. This practice stands in stark contrast to professional problem solving, where the problem comes first, and is a catalyst for investigation and learning. Problem-based learning provides students with an opportunity to grapple with realistic, ill-structured problems using the same kinds of techniques and habits of mind professionals use. The problem-based curriculum and instruction design puts students in the role of professional problem solvers by designing instruction around the investigation of an ill-structured problem. Teachers act as metacognitive coaches and tutors instead of "experts" who have the "right answer" to the problem. Two different applications of problem-based learning at the Illinois Mathematics and Science Academy are described in this article. One application is in an interdisciplinary senior elective course entitled Science, Society and the Future where problems investigate modern dilemmas resulting in modern advances in science and technology; the other is in a more traditional sophomore required course, American Studies, where the problems studied provide students with a feel for the critical decisions which drove the development of the Nation. A description of research projects underway to document the effectiveness of the program is also provided.

The doctors in room A137 look concerned. They have just been handed the file on Jane Barton, who is pregnant with a child who has a condition called anencephally. In a very short time they will have to give Jane their best summary of the baby's condi-

From *Journal for the Education of the Gifted*, Vol. 16, No. 4, 1993, pp. 338–357.
Copyright © 1993 Prufrock Press, Waco, TX. Reprinted with permission.

tion, the potential ramifications of the condition, and the options that Jane and her husband Ralph might want to consider. That means these doctors have a lot of information to gather but not much time. Briefly they consult with each other to organize their thinking and then get to work. They start at the beginning: what the heck is anencephally? What causes it? Will the baby live? What is the risk to Jane? Is abortion still an option? Is it legal? How far is Jane in her pregnancy? What impact will this baby have on the family financially? Say, speaking of money, do they have insurance? What is the hospital's position on abortion and/or taking uninsured patients? Even if the fetus has no chance for survival, can some good come of the situation? What is the doctor's ethical responsibility: do all options, even personally unacceptable ones, have to be presented? Some of these questions may seem simplistic for a group of MDs, until you realize that these "doctors" are gifted high school students in the midst of a course which uses *problem-based learning* to investigate current issues involving the complex interaction of science and society.

Down the hall, American Studies students are in a circle analyzing population figures for the Jamestown settlement during the last three years. It is 1619 and the students, as directors of the company that has established the settlement, are trying to decide on the magnitude and elements of the problem that faces them. The questions students raise as they study the dismal population figures they gathered the day before are thoughtful and probing:

> How many people left England each year for Jamestown?
> How many were men, women or children?
> Did we prepare them for what they would encounter?
> What is the survival rate? What accounts for the high number of deaths?

Later, they broach larger and equally important issues:

> How are we recruiting and encouraging people to go to the New World? What will happen when the news of the hardships is publicized?
> Is the king going to let us keep our charter in Jamestown if people keep dying like this?
> How can we improve the situation so that we can stay in business?

The concentration and involvement in both rooms is intense as students consider what they need to learn to solve their respective problems. As the list of learning issues evolves, students begin to organize themselves to work efficiently as a group to gather the necessary information. Later, heated debates will take place as they use this new knowledge to craft a "best possible" solution. These are just some of the hallmarks of an exciting approach to instruction called *problem-based learning.*

The Center for Problem-Based Learning at the Illinois Mathematics and Science Academy (IMSA) was established as a result of the success of experimental implementation of problem-based learning in two very different settings. Science, Society and the Future (SSF); a semester-long elective course for seniors that focuses on unresolved science-related issues impacting on society causing significant concern for ethical behavior, is interdisciplinary and team-taught exclusively

> ... students begin to organize themselves to work efficiently as a group ...

through the use of *ill-structured* problems. In American Studies, a required year-long course for sophomores that examines the development of institutions, values, and ideas on the North American continent since the arrival of Europeans to North America, problem-based learning takes the form of "post holes" featuring principally interdisciplinary (social sciences plus history) content.

Interest in the use of problem-based learning at IMSA came from two sources. The first was the decades old interest in developing higher level thinking associated with solving problems, making decisions, or thinking critically about societal issues that has been described as "reflective" thinking, "scientific" inquiry, or critical thinking by numerous writers, and which manifested itself in the curriculum and instruction reforms in the 1960s and 1970s in social studies, science, and mathematics. During the 1980s, the literature on thinking exploded around topics such as deductive and inductive reasoning, concrete and abstract thinking, expert and novice problem solvers, stages of moral development, ethics education, collaborative learning, metacognitive skills, well- and ill-structured problems, habits of mind, and general models of intelligence. The scholarship in many of these areas is summarized in Mayer (1983), Covington (1987), Greeno (1989), Resnick (1987), Kohlberg (1981), Costa (1985), Nickerson, Perkins, & Smith (1985), and Voss (1989). The second catalyst for considering the opportunities problem-based learning might offer for the development of higher level thinking skills in secondary school classrooms came from the work of Dr. Howard Barrows in restructuring medical education at Canadian and American medical schools (Barrows, 1985). Barrows noted that medical school graduates left their programs with lots of facts but with little skill in the kind of behaviors and strategies associated with applying information to a diagnosis. He has been successful in organizing a medical school curriculum around the use of ill-structured problems, using them as the catalyst for developing extensive medical knowledge, personalized problem-solving skills, and internal motivation toward inquiry as a life-long habit. Characteristics of the ill-structured problems are as follows:

> More information than is initially available is needed to
> (a) understand the situation/problem, and
> (b) decide what actions are required for resolution, if any.

> Since every problem and problem solver is unique, there is no absolutely right way or fixed formula for conducting an investigation.

> As new information is obtained, the problem changes.

> Students can never be 100% sure they have made the "right" decision because important information may be lacking, data or values may be in conflict, but *decisions have to be made.* (Barrows, 1985)

What is Problem-Based Learning?

Assume that educators took the oft-mentioned goal of "developing problem solvers" or "promoting critical thinking" seriously. That is, they really wanted to help their students become problem solvers, armed with a functioning set of skills that could be activated (and a disposition to want to activate those skills) to sense and define problems, create working hypotheses, gather and analyze data, synthesize findings into solutions, and evaluate or justify those solutions for application into the real world. What would instruction look like in schools with a strong commitment to problem solving? How would course organization change? What would teacher behavior be like? What would students learn? How would learner assessment be conducted? What if we weren't content to just talk about problems or satisfied when our students only recalled what the "experts" have

decided to be solutions, but actually *confronted* students with significant problems, historical and contemporary, domain specific (if it is
possible to relegate a real-life problem to a
single domain of knowledge) or interdisciplinary, ill-structured and messy as they come to
us in the real world? What would happen is
that students would learn to *solve problems* instead of *learning about* problem solving! Instruction would look like it does at IMSA
during problem-based learning episodes.

> What would
> instruction look like
> in schools with a
> strong commitment
> to problem solving?

    Most problem-solving programs present
students with sterile heuristics; very frequently the heuristic takes the
front seat and is considered more important than the problem the
heuristic is meant to help solve. In real life, techniques used to solve
the problem are *dependent on the problem;* its structure; its subject,
its context. Professional problem solvers are adept in selecting strategies appropriate to the problem as the need arises; they do not follow
the lock-stepped proscriptions of a particular problem-solving program. *Program-based learning is apprenticeship for real-life problem
solving.* Instead of tidy case studies typical of more traditional problem-solving programs, students find a situation with undefined
problems, incomplete information, and unasked questions. The scenarios presented to the students demand problem solving the way we
find it in life: defining and detailing issues, creating hypotheses,
searching for and then scanning data, refining hypotheses with the
help of the collected data, conducting empirical experiments or
other research, developing solutions that fit the conditions of the
problem, and then evaluating and/or justifying their solutions so
there is reason to expect conditions will improve. In the process, the
paths of the students' search criss-cross domains of knowledge that
relate to the problem, replete with connections. Students move forward, hit dead ends, go back and revisit data, revise their revisions,
choose a new path and move on. During the process they build substantial knowledge bases through increasingly self-directed study,
structured around the topics of their inquiry—their problem.
Through this kind of real collaboration with their classmates, students refine and enlarge what they know, storing their new knowledge in long term memory and holding it in structures that promote

ESSENCE

transfer to new problems. As the students move toward solutions, they identify *values* that bear on the situation and attend to conflicting *ethical appeals*. And when it is time for resolution (either because the investigators are satisfied with their work, or, as is often the case in the real world, time has "run out" for the problem solvers and a solution is expected—usually demanded—by constituents in the problem situation) solutions are presented, justified and debated until an unacceptable situation (the problem) is made *more acceptable* (sometimes the most we can expect from real-world problem solving). In the process, students become "decidedly different" learners.

Problem-Based Learning in Science, Society and the Future and American Studies

Science, Society and the Future

During the 1988–89 school year, a team of instructors representing Social Science, Physics, and Mathematics, began to design a course that would confront high school seniors with the social and ethical questions inherent in resolving problems and making public policy around controversial scientific issues. The course became reality in 1989 with the aid of a grant from the Hitachi Foundation and *Science, Society and the Future (SSF)* has been team taught as an interdisciplinary elective ever since. The semester-long topics have included "Possible Health Effects of Extremely Low Frequency Radiation," "Biomedical Issue in Life, Death, and Personhood," and "Designing Health Care Systems for the 21st Century." Specific problems are selected based on content goals for the course, with instructors carefully mapping out the areas of content that students will have to "run into" in order to develop a resolution to the problem.

In *SSF*, the problem, ill-structured to resemble the nature of problems as they occur in the real world, comes before all else. Literally! After a few minutes devoted to administrative detail during the first class period of the course, students encounter their first problem.

Jane's Baby, taken from the most recent *SSF* course, is an example of an ill-structured problem. The students receive the problem as it is shown in Figure 1. They are asked to take the role of the "stakeholder" described at the top of the page, namely that of a physician/administrator at a large city hospital. Assuming a stake in the situation forces the students to recognize the roles *perception* and

---

Figure 1
Ill-Structured Scenario, Jane's Baby,
for Science Society and the Future

You are the head of pediatrics at a large city hospital. Jane Barton is one of your patients. Doctor, what will you do in the case of Jane's baby?

Jane Barton is pregnant. She first came to you about two weeks after she and her husband received the results of tests ordered by her family doctor. The tests indicate that Jane and Ralph's baby is anencephalic. The couple is concerned about the fetus and wonder what to do if Jane cannot deliver a normal, healthy infant.

---

responsibility play in problem definition and resolution. Working on the situation from the physician's perspective, responsible to himself for the satisfaction of his own moral and ethical needs as well as those of the profession, hospital and patient, distinguishes this stakeholder from other important participants in the situation such as Jane's parents, either Jane or Ralph as individuals, or even that of the couple's family doctor who might have a very different perception of the couple's emotional needs as compared with that of a specialist at a medical center. In any case, assigning a stake forces students to define the problem within a set of parameters that separates realistic problem solving from that too often used in classrooms, problem solving without a specific perspective or responsibility for the problem solver, typified by a problem statement such as: "What should be done about severely handicapped babies?" Questions which inevitably arise from the ambiguity in the ill-structured situation will lead students to a reiterative process of speculation, problem definition, information gathering, analysis and problem redefinition several times before the problem is resolved.

After reading the handout, the students are asked to list what they know about the situation on the chalkboard under a heading of "What do we know?" Information, always limited as we encounter problems for the first time in the real world, is available primarily in the form of "prior knowledge" accumulated by every student through formal study and from life's experiences. As information is gathered and discussed, the students are asked if a problem exists. If it does, they are asked to describe it *from the perspective of their stake.*

A tentative, hesitant version of a problem statement usually results from this first examination of information. As information is collected, gaps and conflicts within the data are noted. A second list is started on the chalkboard labeled "What do we need to know?" Under this heading are listed the questions that will guide the first out-of-class data gathering assignment. Figure 2 shows a somewhat truncated version of how a chalkboard might look at the end of the first class. The list of questions is analyzed and revised by the group until they are satisfied that they represent the exact questions that need answering. The questions must also be reasonable enough in their scope so that significant progress can be made toward an answer within the time allotted for the search. At the end of class, small groups or individual students volunteer and are assigned individual questions from the list. It is the students' responsibility to answer their questions before they meet again. It is the teachers' responsibility to answer those questions that ask about the simulated lives of the characters in the problem. For example, students investigate questions like: What is anencephaly? Can the mother have trouble delivering an anencephalic baby? What is the prognosis for an anencephalic baby? Is abortion possible for Jane and Ralph? The *SSF* teachers are responsible for information answering questions like: How old is Jane? How long has she been pregnant? What are the couple's religious beliefs? Will the hospital allow abortions in their facility?

Information is gathered from materials in the school's library and from *mentors* in the surrounding community who have been contacted in advance and have agreed to talk with students at specific times on the phone. The information which describes the simulated environment is developed by the teaching team, with help from the mentors if needed, before the course or class begins. Information enters the situation as the students demand it, not in a proscribed "scope and sequence" order. Teachers curb their temptation to problem solve for the students. They do not *tell* the students what they should ask for, what they should think about the data, or how to resolve conflicts within the information. Reflections are restricted to modeling and commenting about metacognition, analyzing the students' questioning process and making students aware of these "executive control" functions. These comments are reserved for strategic places along the path to resolution. Teachers also monitor classroom discussion in their roles as "gate-keepers." They offer the

Figure 2
Sample of Learning Issues Emerging from First Analysis of Jane's Baby

What do we know?

Jane Barton is pregnant.

Jane is married.

Medical tests indicate that her fetus is anencephalic.

Jane and Ralph feel that their baby might not be normal.

Jane has been referred by another doctor.

Anencephalic babies don't survive.

It has something to do with the brain.

What do we need to know?

What is the medical description of anencephally?

What is Jane's general health?

Does she have children?

What test did she have? How accurate is it?

Is abortion possible in this case?

What is the law on abortion in our state?

How do Jane and Ralph feel about abortion?

Are there alternatives to abortion in this case?

How long do anencephalic babies live?

What is their "quality of life?"

What are the religious beliefs of the Bartons?

What causes anencephally?

What effect does anencephally have on future pregnancies?

Can fetal organs and tissues be used?

What should we do?

Order another test to confirm the diagnosis.

Discuss the condition of the fetus with the Bartons before too long.

Have technology ready to help the baby at birth.

Use the tissue/organs of the fetus in some way.

floor to students having difficulty breaking into the conversation but do *not* control its content. If refocusing is in order, the teacher might make metacognitive observations. But responsibility for *productivity* rests with the students—the problem solvers.

When new information is brought to class, it is evaluated for its reliability and usefulness and then used to modify the problem statement, if necessary. As each student gathers information and thinks about the data, true collaboration develops within the class as students listen and react to thoughts brought to the discussion by other students holding unique information based upon their own fact finding.

> **When new information is brought to class, it is evaluated for its reliability and usefulness and then used to modify the problem statement, if necessary.**

As the base of medical, legal, economic, ethical/moral, and situation-specific information is enlarged, the problem definition is finalized (although always considered tentative so new information can be accommodated) and hypotheses about what can or should be done are formulated. Students then use their creative skills and their ability to analyze and synthesize as they propose elements for resolution of the problem. Again new data may be needed. If some, it is collected, evaluated, applied and the hypotheses are strengthened, modified or discarded altogether. As with most of life's ill-structured problems, the problem solvers do *not* have an unlimited time to resolve the issue. Solutions must be offered even when the data is incomplete, in conflict or includes conflicting ethical appeals. In the problem of Jane's baby, Jane's pregnancy is moving along and some solution options can disappear as her fetus develops. Besides, each of the students has *an assessment*—an appointment with the Bartons—coming up soon and they must be ready to help the couple with their problem when the time comes—and the time often comes much too quickly from the student's point of view!

The visit with the Bartons, played by volunteers from the surrounding community or the IMSA faculty and staff, marks "decision time" for the students. It is during this fifteen minute "consultation" that students are usually confronted with two aspects of the problem that were not evident until they said "Hello" to their patients. The first has to do with the relationship between physician and patient during the decision making. More specifically, *who* should make this decision? The second has to do with the communication skills necessary to help the patient understand the options and risks that are inherent in each possible solution. The *SSF* teachers prepare each of the "Barton couples" to ask the questions that will help illustrate the quality of the preparation by the physicians.

Each interview is observed by an *SSF* teacher and the physician's performance is evaluated according to criteria shared with the students well before they met their patients. Observations on the consultations are shared with the class during a debriefing period and the information from the observations is added to that gathered through evaluation of the *problem logs*, completed by each student as the case of Jane's baby unfolded. The problem log is a journal-type record of the development of the problem. Specific assignments planned for the log help instructors keep track of students' thinking; notes kept by students independent of the assignment help students take advantage of sudden insights which may be helpful to the group. The log also helps students develop and recognize the habits of mind associated with problem solving. A series of problem-log activities might take a form like this:

> **Log Exercise 1.** Based on your current understanding of Jane's situation, create a statement of the problem.
>
> **Log Exercise 2.** Provide a medical description of anencephally.
>
> **Log Exercise 3.** Describe the ethical dilemma(s) involved in the problem of Jane's baby.
>
> **Log Exercise 4.** Now that you have researched and discussed this problem, how would you advise Jane and Ralph?
>
> **Log Exercise 5.** What did you learn from your interview with the Bartons? How, if at all, did this experience change your perception of the problem?

The resolution of the Barton's problem leads into another investigation. The physicians have learned that the Bartons would like to make something good out of the very tragic situation involving Jane's fetus and have asked if tissue or organs from the fetus can be donated to research after the baby is aborted or after it is delivered and dies, usually a matter of a few days in the case of anencephalic infants. Research into this issue unveils the existence of an

executive order from the Regan White House forbidding the use of
fetal tissue from elective abortions in research at any institution
receiving federal funds. After the resolution
of the Barton's situation, the students are
recast in the role of congressmen faced with
legislation intent on overturning the existing
executive order. As this problem unfolds, students investigate the potential impact of fetal
tissue research on medical science, the position held by the two major political parties on
the issue, what special interest groups think
about the situation, and the status of fetal
tissue research in other countries, among
many other things. As the information base
grows, amendments and competing legisla-
tion drafted by the student legislators enter the situation. When students ask about the feelings of the current White House on the issue,
they telephone the White House staff and other agencies to request
information. The role of politics in medical research soon becomes
apparent.

> Students need to
> plunge right in to see
> life's problems as
> usually complex, not
> simple, requiring the
> use of data from
> critical inquiry in
> order to understand
> the problems . . .

Criss-crossing the domains of medical ethics, fetal tissue research and technology's impact on life and death decisions (later
situations in the *SSF* course focused on knotty issues involving quality of life, technology, and end of life issues) is done in order to increase *cognitive flexibility* (Spiro, Visopoel, Schmitz, Samarapugavan,
& Boerger, 1989), to remove the oversimplified generalization held
by many high school students that one need only consider the obvious when solving problems, and establish the attitude that one must
consider the interrelatedness of domains of knowledge and point of
view when attempting to understand and solve ill-structured problems. If skill in solving problems is to be developed in high school
students, we must not stop at the water's edge, simply looking at the
sea of problems. Students need to plunge right in to see life's problems as usually complex, not simple, requiring the use of data from
critical inquiry in order to understand the problems and fashion
workable solutions. Further, they should consider the impact of
solutions before advocating them and be able to communicate
effectively their scholarship and thinking throughout the process.

Post-Holing in American Studies, Science Society and the Future is entirely problem driven. The first problem is initiated on the first day of class and the last problem in the linked series of problems is the "final exam" for the course. It uses problem-based learning for all it's worth. In contrast, problem-based American Studies uses a number of ill-structured problems as a post-holes, short problems which interrupt more typical instruction during a unit, while continuing to employ more traditional methodologies where "coverage" is desired.

American Studies is an interdisciplinary course, combining content from history and the social sciences, that explores major themes in the evolution of American society. The course is required for all sophomores at the Illinois Mathematics and Science Academy. A number of themes in American Studies, listed in Figure 3, have been taught using ill-structured problems as post-holes since 1989.

Figure 3
Organizational Themes for American Studies

Becoming "Americans"

Power and the Framework for Government

The Continuing Revolution; Rights in America

America's Rise to a World Power

Post-holing describes a curriculum organizational pattern that balances "coverage" of the themes in the course with problem-based investigations using the same process as *Science, Society and the Future* but with content rooted more firmly in history and the social sciences. A post-hole consists of a series of days within a unit which are devoted to *depth of understanding* rather than *content coverage*. Designed around ill-structured problems, post-holes are times when instruction changes from traditional methodologies like source reading and discussion or lecturette (selected because of their efficiency in helping students acquire information) to problem-based behaviors and investigations. As in *SSF*, the problems are ill-structured and students are asked to confront the situations as problem solvers within a given historical context. The objective of these problems is not to discover what really happened in the situation or resolve a question of fact or theory (as is the goal of instruction typically described as "inquiry") but to resolve problems using data and, hopefully, mind sets consistent with the places, characters, events and chronology found in each problem situation.

Therefore, as members of the Board of Directors of the Virginia Company, students are faced with a challenge by the King of England to convince him that the Virginia colony should be given another charter in light of its performance to date, 1619. The students determine the goals of the company and those of the crown for the promotion of the colony through investigation of the first two characters for the colony, the writings on mercantilism by the Hakluyts, maps and writings by Englishmen from the sixteenth and early seventeenth century. From these documents they identify factors that might make up a "push and pull" for migration to the New World, and then reflectively assemble a case for keeping control of the colony in the hands of the company while new policies toward population stabilization and growth, generating increased revenue for the company and the crown, and generally improving the likelihood that the colony will succeed are designed and implemented by the Board. The object is to require the students to problem solve from the perspective and with the responsibilities of a London businessman on the board of the Virginia Company.

Later in the course, under the theme of America's rise to world power, students are asked to advise President Truman on a strategy to end the war in the Pacific. The problem they face is contained in a very brief memo they each receive from Secretary of War Stimson which contains the operative sentence:

> "The president is most anxious to receive your recommendations on how to bring a speedy end to the war, based upon unconditional surrender by the Japanese, and providing for a secure post war world."

When students arrive for the next class meeting, the first meeting of their "interim committee," they are given a TOP SECRET briefing sheet on the recent denotation of an atomic bomb on the reservation at Los Alamos, New Mexico. Problem solving begins with the teacher/tutor asking the committee members, "What can you tell the committee about our situation on July 18, 1945, (the date on the top of the memo from the President)?" By the end of the

class period, the students have shared their knowledge on the state of
the world and the war in the summer of 1945. More importantly,
they have identified questions they need to answer about issues facing the warring parties. These questions include:

> How is the war going in the Pacific?
> How do American and Japanese casualties compare in the most recent
>   battles?
> What do we know about the Japanese mentality and the conduct of
>   warfare?
> How successful has our blockade and bombing been in slowing the
>   Japanese war effort?
> How many atomic bombs does the US have? What will it be like to use
>   this weapon in combat?
> What did the bomb cost?
> How do the Russians and Americans feel about each other at this
>   point in the war?
> Will Russia enter the war against Japan? If so, when? What will Russia
>   want in return for participating?
> Why must we have unconditional surrender?
> What is Allied morale like in the field?
> Does America have an invasion plan? What is it like? What will the
>   invasion cost in lives?

The first class meeting closes with students being assigned one
of the above questions and they are directed to the library to find
materials that might be helpful for their investigation. The following
three or four class sessions are devoted to enlarging "what we know"
about the situation in the Pacific, counting largely on collaboration
between learners, each student responsible for finding information
and sharing it as the discussion demands. As the data gathering,
sharing, and analysis develop, the teacher begins to ask the class to
build strategy options that seem feasible to them. Finally, based upon
a request from the President that the committee forward its recommendations immediately, the class/committee must turn its complete attention to strategy formation. Options are developed in
detail, strengths and weaknesses of each are considered in light of
the three criteria identified in the President's original request, and a
consensus option is built. Minority opinions are also attached to the
final recommendations.

Now that the class has a recommendation for the President,
they are faced with justifying their choice. This is done in one of two

ways. The teacher may change roles to become the President and press the students to justify their strategy in the face of the tough questions facing Truman in 1945. Alternately, students could demonstrate their thinking about their choice by writing a rationale as the last activity in their "problem log." As a part of the log for this problem, the students will have already (1) written a problem definition after the first class discussion, (2) identified an especially useful source from the library, and (3) prepared a preliminary strategy recommendation. Each of these entries is evaluated by the teacher and used to help determine a grade for the students at the end of the problem.

> A need was clearly apparent to establish problem-based learning as more than a "gee-whiz-doesn't-this-look-neat" curriculum adaptation.

RESEARCH AND EVALUATION

From the beginning, the team of instructors experimenting with problem-based curriculum and instruction recognized the need to evaluate the success of the technique. A need was clearly apparent to establish problem-based learning as more than a "gee-whiz-doesn't-this-look-neat" curriculum adaptation. The entire project team was convinced that the problem-based approach represented the ideal setting for combining the best of metacognitive and "thinking skills" instruction with rigorous, meaningful content. Research and evaluation topics identified for study were numerous and fell into a few basic categories, including 1) changes in problem-solving skills, 2) effectiveness in teaching content knowledge, and 3) students' perception of their learning in the courses. These three areas of inquiry represent a sizable and on-going agenda for research and evaluation; results from only a few preliminary projects can currently be reported. Projects selected for initial research were chosen, in part, to match the two different instructional environments. Research in *SSF* has concentrated on student cognition, including changes in problem solving, use of different ethical appeals when problem solving, and more qualitative reactions to the overall approach to the course. Research in the American Studies class has focused exclusively on the relative effectiveness of problem-based curriculum and instruction to transmit traditional factual content to students.

Research in Science, Society and the Future

As an elective and completely problem-driven course, evaluation in *SSF* has focused primarily on problem solving and student reactions to the course. To test the relative effectiveness of problem-based curriculum in improving problem solving, students in the *SSF* class were given a pre- and post-test problem-solving activity. The activity presented an ill-structured problem to the students, who were instructed to outline the procedures they would use to arrive at a resolution to the problem. Students from a separate senior elective course (psychology) were given the same pre- and post-test to serve as a comparison group. Analysis of the data from the two groups of students revealed a significant increase in the use of *problem finding* by *SSF* students. No similar increase was observed among students in the comparison group. A complete description of this study can be found in Gallagher, Stepien, and Rosenthal (1992).

In the second year of *SSF,* attention was turned to the question of the number of ethical appeals that students use when considering ambiguous moral dilemmas. For instance, do they consider just personal rights, or also the rights of others, justice, personhood? Again, students in the *SSF* class were pre- and post-tested along with a comparison group. Again, the students in the *SSF* class showed modifications in the breadth of ethical appeals considered after the course, unlike the comparison group whose considerations remained consistent from pre-test to post-test. Interestingly, the students showed little tendency to actually change their stance on an issue such as abortion or euthanasia, instead, they tended to extend their support of their appeal from mostly emotional to emotion substantiated by reason.

Not all meaningful data is statistical; equally important to the implementation team were more subjective reactions of students to the *SSF* course. Students in the first year of the *SSF* class were asked to complete a questionnaire soliciting their reactions to three key questions: 1) What have you learned about problem solving? 2) Do you think you can transfer what you learned to new situations? and 3) What did you think about the course? In an interesting parallel to the statistical data gathered in the problem-solving activity students often referred to an increased (or brand new) understanding of the need to engage in problem finding prior to engaging in problem solving. Students' responses also reflected a greater appreciation for the vagaries and nuances of real-world problem solving.

I learned how research works. There are no answers. There is no book you can go to look up the effect. Everything must be analyzed carefully. Overlooking the slightest detail can be disastrous.

I now know that voluminous amounts of information must be collected and analyzed before any rational person will take responsibiltiy for any action, even maintaining status quo, in real-life situations. I now know that analysis of information is more important than accumulation of data. I now know that "lucky guesses" are few and far between; much time is saved by not relying on or expecting them.

The most important step I learned was that the existence of a problem needs to be detemined before any decisions can be made on how to deal with it. If there is a problem, it must be clearly defined, since too often we can concentrate on looking for solutions to the wrong problem. Sometimes problems have no clear, right-or-wrong solutions, unlike most "classroom problems," it may be frustrating but it is often the case, and we must learn to deal with it.

What may seem obviously wrong may possibly be right. Solutions are not 100% satisfactory most of the time. There is usually more than one best answer/solution. The idea of what is mostly right differs from person to person. Life is full of gray areas. Sometimes we just have to live with the risks because the benefits are much greater.

These qualitative statements provide substantive demonstrations of the power of this instructional approach to teach students some of the "intangibles" of problem solving. What has provided a more independent source of information has been the longitudinal study of IMSA graduates. Each year IMSA graduates are contacted by telephone and asked to reflect about various aspects of the program. Included among the questions are inquiries about the students' favorite course, and about the course which was most effective in increasing problem finding, problem solving, critical thinking and ethical decision making. Responses from the class of 1990, the first group of students to be offered *SSF* as an elective alternative, clearly and overwhelming favored *SSF* on each of these questions (Gallagher, 1991).

Research in American Studies
In American Studies a study was conducted which was considered critical to establishing the viability of problem-based instruction for gifted students in secondary school. Often approaches in pedagogy which digress from a traditional didactic or read-and-discuss methodology are avoided because of the fear that using more open-ended,

inquiry based techniques are not capable of transferring critical factual content necessary for responsible preparation for college. This assumption was tested in the American Studies class through a pre-test and post-test of factual content in American Studies. Students in the course with problem-based post-holes as well as students in more traditional American Studies courses at the Academy were tested before and after the course using traditional end-of-chapter questions from a well-reputed American Studies textbook. The results, which are reported in more detail elsewhere (Gallagher, Stepien, & Stepien, in

> A series of additional projects indicate that this method is engaging and effective for students even younger than high school.

preparation), showed that the students in the problem-based courses gained as much, if not more, factual content that students in IMSA American Studies courses organized around more traditional instruction. Considered a very important preliminary finding, this study is currently being replicated with the addition of students in traditional Advanced Placement American History courses in classrooms outside of the Academy.

Taken together, the results of the research efforts associated with the integration of problem-based curriculum into the curriculum shows great promise. Certainly much more research will be needed, especially testing for long-term effectiveness, and measurement of in increase in motivation, self-efficacy and excitement that students in the problem-based environment exhibit as they are finally allowed to abandon the predictable problems of textbooks and tests and take the role of responsible problem solver, just as they know they will as professionals.

THE FUTURE OF PROBLEM-BASED LEARNING

A series of additional projects indicate that this method is engaging and effective for students even younger than high school. At the College of William and Mary, a curriculum contract awarded by the Department of Education was fulfilled by creating eight problem-based science units; during field testing all instructors commented on how effectively the approach "turned students on" to science in second through seventh grade classes. A special summer program for minority gifted students from the city of Chicago demonstrated that the technique provided minority students with a motivating and stimulating environment for learning in an interdisciplinary context. Taken together, the initial results of all our projects provide the data necessary to continue our efforts at refining and expanding the application of problem-based learning strategies to the secondary school curriculum. As the Center for Problem-Based Learning continues to develop and grow, we hope to see the technique tested with more and more different settings, subject disciplines, and student populations. Right now, the future of problem-based learning seems limited only to the imagination and initiative of teachers who experiment with the process.

Acknowledgments: We would like to express our gratitude to the following IMSA personnel for their assistance in the current projects: Stephanie Pace Marshall, Executive Director; Susan Eddins, Mathematics; Christian Nokkentved, Social Science, Hilary Rosenthal, Social Science; and William C. Stepien, Research Assistant. Inquiries about the Center for Problem Based Learning or reprints of this article should be sent to William J. Stepien, IMSA, 1500 W. Sullivan Road, Aurora, IL 60506-1039.

REFERENCES

Barrows, H. (1985). *How to design a problem-based learning curriculum in the preclinical years.* New York: Springer-Verlag.

Costa, A. (Ed.). (1985). *Developing minds: A resource book for teaching thinking.* Alexandria, VA: Association for Supervision and Curriculum Development.

Covington, L. (1987). Instruction in problem-solving planning. In S. Friedman, E. Scholnick, and R. Cocking (Eds.), *Blueprints for thinking: The role of planning in cognitive development.* Cambridge University Press, 469–511.

Gallagher, S. (1991). Longitudinal study of IMSA graduates: Class of 1990. Presentation made the IMSA Board of Trustees, Aurora, Illinois, November.

Gallagher, S., Stepien, W., & Stepien, W. (in preparation). The effect of problem-based learning on acquisition of facts in American Studies.

Gallagher, S., Stepien, W., & Rosenthal, H. (1992). The effects of problem-based leaning on problem solving. *Gifted Child Quarterly, 36* (4), 195–200.

Greeno, J. (1989). A perspective on thinking. *American Psychologist, 44* (2), 131–141.

Kohlberg, L. (1981). *The philosophy of moral development: Moral stages and the idea of justice.* NY: Harper and Row.

Mayer, R. (1983). *Thinking, problem solving, cognition.* NY: W. H. Freeman.

Nickerson, R., Perkins, D., & Smith, E. (1985). *The teaching of thinking.* Hillsdale, NJ: Lawrence Erlbaum Associates.

Resnick, L. (1987). *Education and learning to think.* Washington, DC: National Academy Press.

Spiro, R., Vispoel, W., Schmitz, J., Samarapugavan, A., & Boerger, A. (1987). Knowledge acquisitions for application: Cognitive flexibility and transfer in complex content domains. In B. Britton (Ed.), *Executive control processes.* Hillsdale, NJ: Lawrence Erlbaum Associates.

Voss, J. (1989). Problem solving and the educational process. In R. Glaser and A. Lesgold (Eds.), *Foundations for a psychology of education.* Hillsdale, NJ: Lawrence Erlbaum Associates.

This Is a Messy Job, but Somebody's Got to Do It!

by Erica Pearson

The student grinned as she and her friend wrestled with marshmallows and toothpicks and tried to make their slowly emerging sphere stand up. The marshmallows were messy, but so was the problem: in 30 minutes, using only 50 toothpicks and up to 50 small marshmallows, make the largest sphere possible.

In real life, problems are messy. Think of the engineers in the movie *Apollo 13,* who raced the clock to make round carbon dioxide scrubbers fit into square holes. The lives the astronauts depended on the engineers and their ingenuity for there was no ready-made solution to the problem. Finding the answer took teamwork, flexible thinking, trial-and-error experimentation at breakneck speed, and lots of duct tape.

Engineers, inventors, designers and scientists, business people, doctors, lawyers, and teachers all solve problems daily. They bring their past learning to new problems, but they are often faced with situations for which there are no clear precedents. They must take risks, make decisions, and refine their understanding by observing the results of their actions.

It is possible to simulate these conditions for our students. Many teachers of gifted students are investigating problem-based learning. They hope to help their pupils become life-long learners, and to encourage the practice of skills that will be essential in adulthood. These include interpersonal skills such as teamwork, negotiation, and communication, as well as intrapersonal skills and attitudes such as risk-taking, tolerance for ambiguity and frustration, perseverance, and creative and critical thinking. The design of problem-based learning also allows students to practice the higher level thinking skills of analysis, synthesis, and evaluation in integrated, real-life activities.

Problem-based learning can take the form of long-term projects based on extensive student research. But it can also take the form of short problem-solving experiences that take only 30 to 45 minutes from start to finish. These can be an excellent way to introduce students to open-ended, messy problems, for which there are many good answers instead of a single correct one. These exercises can also be a good way for interested teachers to try the concept of problem-based learning in miniature, and to make modifications based on the reactions of their students, before they commit themselves to major projects.

The following activities (development in 1986 by Ron Lewin, technology consultant for schools in Berkshire, England) were tested by fourth grade students in the LOGOS gifted and talented pull-out program in Richmond, IN.

CARDBOARD TOWER

Materials (per group)
1 9" x 12" piece of colored posterboard, 2 9" x 12" pieces of white posterboard, 1 roll of masking tape, and scissors

Problem
In 30 minutes, make a free-standing structure which is as tall as possible. You may use the white board to test your design. The final product must be constructed with the colored board.

PLASTIC CUP BRIDGE

Materials (per group)
24 plastic cups, 1 pair of scissors per person

Problem
In 30 minutes, using only cutting and slotting methods, make a structure with a single, supporting cup at each end and the maximum span possible.

PAPER FLOATER

Materials (per group)
sheet of paper, multiple sheets for practice, tape, paper clips, scissors

Problem

In 30 minutes, make a device from a single sheet of paper (all of the sheet must be used) which, when dropped from a height of two meters, will take as long as possible to free-fall to the ground.

EXTENDED ARM

Materials (per group)
newspapers, 1 roll of masking tape, scissors

Problem

In 30 minutes, make a free-standing structure that will reach out as far as possible from a fixed point and remain stable.

MESSY SPHERE

Materials (per group)
50 toothpicks, 50 small marshmallows

Problem

In 30 minutes, make the largest sphere you can. (For the mathematically inclined, try to estimate or calculate the volume of the completed sphere.)

When the 30 minutes for each project were up, the class was called together to go from one work-station to the next, viewing each other's projects, and listening to each group's account of the problems it faced, and the solutions it found. Students were then asked to write individual accounts of the project, including their feelings about it.

It was interesting to observe the changes in the children's attitudes and behavior as they worked on the projects each week. The reaction of many to the first project (the cardboard tower) was negative—they felt competitive, frustrated over lack of access to the materials, frustrated about communicating with their teammates, frustrated by what they perceived as failure; so frustrated that some just wanted to give up. For example, several groups immediately cut up their cardboard into small pieces and tried to create structures that looked like skyscrapers or step-pyramids. When they noticed that one group had made a simple cylinder using the entire length of the cardboard, they were mortified. Quotes from their journals illustrate their feelings.

A: "I hated it, but I stuck with it . . . I didn't really do anything. S. was the bossiest!"

B: "I hated this! . . . We had to think for a while and finally R. came up with this idea. It was our final model."

C: "We went about this project wrong. We looked at it very badly. I wish that we would have gotten our tower bigger. Our group didn't have enough ideas . . . I don't know how my teammates feel about this, but I feel that we at least gave it an effort."

D: "I kind of liked it. I looked over at T.'s table and their tower was built up with one piece of paper. Not to brag but I think I came up with the idea. S. quit and said it would never work . . . I got frustrated too but I didn't give up."

E: "X, did most of the work. I cut the tape. V. balanced it . . . I didn't think of an idea. I didn't like the idea."

F: "X. thought of the tower, but Z. thought about how to support the tower . . . I wish we could at least let me try my idea."

On the basis of these comments and teacher observations of behavior, some changes were made in the second project (Plastic Cup Bridge). For the first project, the students had formed their own groups of four to five members each. For the second, the groups were limited to two members, to minimize competition for materials, and to allow everyone's ideas to be used. This arrangement still required teamwork and cooperation. Boys and girls were paired, to encourage communication across gender barriers and to join students of similar temperament and ability who would be most likely to work as colleagues instead of leaders and followers.

In the introduction to the project, the teacher also emphasized that the activity was neither a contest nor a race. Although they were divided into pairs, the whole class was still a single team. Copying was not prohibited; it was encouraged, as a valuable brainstorming method called "piggybacking." Students were invited to walk around the room as they took breaks from their work, and to use and adapt ideas from the work of other teams. These instructions seemed to decrease the students' anxiety and also their frustration levels. All but one reported enjoying the activity this time, and the animation in their faces and voices as they struggled with recalcitrant pieces of curved plastic substantiated their comments.

Anxiety was further reduced by the teacher's questions and observations as the group viewed each team's effort at the end of the 30 minutes. The unique qualities of each structure were pointed out. Students were encouraged to see the flexibility in each other's approach to the same problem, and the elegance of many different solutions. One pair of students wanted to measure the longest spans for each bridge, but was told that it had to ask each team's permission first.

H: "It was easy. I used an idea from the tower."

J: "Well it seemed like an unidentified flying object. I felt that working on one for a long time pays off. I liked working with K."

L: "I got very frustrated at the beginning, but it got better. M. had an idea where you put a base kind of thing on the support. I thought of using cut-up cups to hold it, and when we put it together it worked. I'm very proud."

M: "I felt real good. The bridge was small but great."

N: "I liked it a lot better. It was a lot more fun, and we only used eight cups and had 16 left."

O: "Personally, I was aggravated with it, but it stood up. To sum it up I hated it."

P: "I had a lot of fun. It was hard at times. It was hard to get our bridge to stay up. We had to really think. I'm proud of what we did!"

Q: "I liked it a lot better. S. and I make a good team! We made two slots in a piece of cup and joined them together. It made a long bridge."

For the third project (Paper Floater), the students were again divided into pairs, but ended up doing their design work as individuals, such the resources (scrap paper and small scissors) were unlimited. They used their partners mostly as sounding boards for ideas and reactions to trial runs.

One boy immediately folded his paper in the shape of a paper airplane. When reminded that his device had to free-fall, not be launched, he was astounded to find that the tip of the plane immediately pointed to the ground which caused it to nose-dive with great speed. Several students began experimenting with cutting slits in the paper, and discovered that there was an optimum slitting level: too few or too many slits both made the paper fall faster. Others designed various sorts of parachutes: rectangular, circular, and cylindrical, with tilted fins at the top to make the paper twirl as it fell. The latter design had to be weighted with paper clips to keep it upright as it descended. One group made a construction with spiraling tendrils like a jellyfish.

All the written reactions were positive again, except for one.

> O: "I was really aggravated. I figured that the best one would hold the most air. I finally did it. And I hated it."

For the fourth project (Extended Arm), the students freely circulated around the classroom, discussing designs in progress with each other, and offering suggestions. One group made paper suspension cables to hold up the longest arm of its construction. Another weighted its central support with many layers of folded newspaper concealed inside a cube-shaped cover. Another discovered that it could increase the strength of its over-long tube arm by folding it in on itself. The group then solved its base's stability problem by compacting it as well. This solution created a sculpture that looked to everyone like a buffalo skull. Students complimented each other on both aesthetics and engineering. The teacher congratulated the entire group for coping with extreme frustration without giving up. If the students' first idea had not worked, they had started again with good humor and energy. Even the most skeptical student decided that these projects were not so bad after all.

> O: "It was better than last time. I wasn't quite as aggravated. The weight on the longest side was a big factor, so we had to make the support wider" (comment accompanied by a diagram, labeled, "the ungodly thing that we made").

The fifth project (Messy Sphere) was greeted with interest and enthusiasm by all the students. One team formed two half-spheres, then joined them together. Another approached the problem geometrically, by making squares with triangles projecting from each side, linking them together, and stablizing the squares with diagonal toothpicks. Other groups experimented with breaking toothpicks, mashing marshmallows to glue sections together, and, when the toothpicks ran out, trying to use towers of marshmallows in their place (that didn't work). They coped with extreme frustration as the soft marshmallows caused their structures to droop and buckle, always threatening to collapse. Some made internal armatures out of crushed paper; others waited for one part to dry and stiffen a bit before attempting to attach it to another. But no one complained or threatened to quit. The complications just seemed to add interest to the challenges they faced.

What was important was the fact that the students all had become confident problem solvers who were ready to take risks, test the properties and limits of their materials, work with trial and error, and see their mistakes not as failures, but as learning opportunities.

By using problem-based learning, both students and the teacher had taken risks, wrestled with messy problems, and learned something new about materials, methods, people, process, and the joy of making discoveries together.

REFERENCE

Lewin, R. (1986). *Technology—first the problem.* Shire Hall, Reading, Berkshire, UK: Berkshire Local Education Authority.

Problem-Based Mathematics— Not Just for the College-Bound

by Lynne Alper, Dan Fendel, Sherry Fraser, and Diane Resek

Mathematics is far more interesting to students when they get to do some real thinking. That is one of the premises of the Interactive Mathematics Program.

Picture this: You're on a planning team, consulting to the city manager. Your task is to come up with a reasonable plan for the use of 550 acres of land recently obtained by the city. The acreage includes a recently closed army base, a 300-acre farm, and abandoned mining land.

Two conflicting parties are interested in the property. The business community is pushing for development schemes, while environmental groups are advocating for recreational space. The two factions have arrived at a partial compromise, which is what you have to work with. They have agreed that

• a maximum of 200 acres from the army base and the mining land will be used for recreation, and

• the amount of army land used for recreation plus the amount of farm land used for development will together total 100 acres.

Not only are you dealing with opposing factions, but with improvement costs ranging from $50 to $2,000 per acre, depending on which parcel of land is involved and how it will be used. You have to satisfy everyone while minimizing the total cost for improvements. To arrive at a reasonable allocation plan will demand careful analysis and attention to detail.

If you were 16 and in a traditional high school math class, you would be enrolled in Algebra II, perhaps doing one system of linear equations after another.

Instead, it's a whole new ball game. Your task is to solve the city's planning problem. This isn't an extra credit assignment. It's a unit called *Meadows or Malls?* You're going to be working on it for the next six to eight weeks, learning and using algebra, geometry, and matrix operations.

> **Don't expect to spend your time memorizing facts.**

Don't expect to spend your time memorizing facts. There will be no pop quizzes, and no columns of figures to work on and turn in when the bell rings.

Do expect to be working both in a group and on your own. You'll be dealing with numbers and doing matrix operations on a sophisticated calculator. You'll also be working with words—writing and explaining to the rest of the class how your group arrived at its solution to the problem.

Welcome to Year 3 of the Interactive Mathematics Program, also known as IMP.

ABOUT THE PROGRAM

The Interactive Mathematics Program is currently funded by the National Science Foundation to design a comprehensive high school mathematics curriculum. It fulfills the vision of *Curriculum and Evaluation Standards for School Mathematics* (National Council of Teachers of Mathematics 1989). Since 1989, IMP has been used in classrooms throughout the United States to develop and test the kinds of tasks sought by NCTM, embedding those tasks within a larger vision of a complete mathematics program. It is one of five programs funded by NSF to develop new comprehensive curriculums at the high school level.

IMP's four-year program replaces the traditional Algebra I-Geometry-Algebra II/Trigonometry-Precalculus sequence. The program integrates traditional material with additional topics recommended by the NCTM Standards, such as probability and statistics, and utilizes graphing calculator technology to enhance student understanding. This new curriculum meets college entrance requirements and prepares students to use problem-solving skills at school and on the job.

Teachers need extensive support when they adopt this curriculum, beginning with inservice workshops. The optimum introductory arrangement also includes scheduling one period per day for new IMP teachers to study and to share experiences. Other forms of support include team-teaching the first year of implementation and maintaining a network of telephone contact among teachers.

We have extensively tested the four-year program, and classroom teachers and curriculum writers have continually reviewed and revised it. The program is scheduled to be published by Key Curriculum Press beginning in fall 1996.

> **While students have both the teacher and their peers as resources, each is expected to think and to create in mathematics class.**

THINKING ABOUT MATHEMATICS

A major premise of the Interactive Mathematics Program is that most students are capable of thinking about mathematics and understanding complex concepts. This is a change from the philosophy of many traditional programs in which students do mostly rote work. The role of the program teacher also differs from that of a traditional mathematics teacher. In IMP, the emphasis is on guiding students and helping them make connections between key mathematical ideas and concepts, while minimizing time spent lecturing to the class. While students have both the teacher and their peers as resources, each is expected to think and to create in mathematics class.

The Interactive Mathematics Program is a problem-based curriculum. For example, each unit, such as *Meadows or Malls?*, begins with a motivating problem, too difficult for almost any of the students to solve at first. Students examine this initial situation and then look at similar, perhaps simpler, situations in shorter problems. At every step along the way, students must pose questions, look for patterns, and make connections between the current problem and the mathematics they have learned in previous units. By solving a variety of problems, students deepen their understanding, and they begin to abstract the concepts and refine the techniques needed to apply to the complex original problem.

In order for a problem to build mathematical power in the student, the student needs the opportunity to do genuine thinking about it. In IMP, this means giving students a chance to explore, conjecture, experiment, and reflect on their results. If students fail initially, they return to the problem for more exploration, new conjectures, and more experimentation. The real thinking in problem solving takes place in examining an unfamiliar situation and finding the underlying mathematical ideas. This will occur only if problems are presented without a fixed procedure or solution.

LEARNING THE BASICS

Both traditional mathematics curriculums and the Interactive Mathematics Program cover basic high school mathematics content. Here are some examples.

1. *Algebra.* Solving systems of linear equations for unknowns is an important skill in traditional algebra classes. In IMP, this topic is presented both in *Meadows or Malls?* and in a second-year unit called *Cookies,* which deals with maximizing profits from a bakery. Students don't just learn one method, but develop their own approaches in groups and then share ideas with one another. In *Meadows or Malls?* they also see how to use matrices and the technology of graphing calculators to solve such systems.

2. *Geometry.* Basic concepts in traditional geometry include similar triangles and the Pythagorean theorem. In *Shadows,* a first-year IMP unit, students learn about similar triangles, develop proportion equations to solve similar triangles, and apply the concept of similarity to predict the lengths of shadows. They also extend their knowledge to see how similarity is used as the foundation of trigonometry.

In *Do Bees Build It Best?* students develop the Pythagorean theorem experimentally, prove it algebraically or geometrically, and apply it to see why the hexagonal prism of the bees' honeycomb design is the most efficient regular prism possible. Several units later, students apply the Pythagorean theorem to develop other principles, such as the distance formula in coordinate geometry.

3. *Trigonometry.* In traditional programs, sine, cosine, and tangent are introduced in the 11th or 12th grade. In IMP, students begin working with these functions in 9th grade (in *Shadows*), and learn their value and application over the years. Right triangle trigonometry is used in several units in the second and third year.

In a fourth-year unit, *High Dive,* students extend trigonometry from right triangles to circular functions, defining the trigonometric functions for angles of more than 90 degrees. The problem-solving context in this unit is a circus act in which a performer jumps off a Ferris wheel into a moving tub of water. Not only are students developing and applying general ideas from trigonometry, but they are also learning principles of physics, developing laws for falling objects, and using vectors to find vertical and horizontal elements of velocity.

> . . . units are complex, innovative, and challenging. Solving them involves a blend of different concepts and techniques.

WORD PROBLEMS WITH A DIFFERENCE

At first glance, a problem like that in *Meadows and Malls?* resembles the word problems of traditional algebra courses. Both take students out of the realm of pure mathematics, requiring them to see the mathematical structure in a real-life situation. Let's ignore the fact that traditional word problems often strike students as contrived and artificial (two trains going in opposite directions from the station, for example). What's more important is the way they are presented.

Generally, in a traditional class, teachers give students a step-by-step procedure for one such problem and then ask them to practice the procedure on problems of exactly the same type. Each category of problem is narrowly designed to rehearse students on a specific skill. The result is that students do not need to solve a problem in the sense of thinking through a new situation. They merely follow a prescription.

By contrast, the central problem in the Interactive Mathematics Program units are complex, innovative, and challenging. Solving them involves a blend of different concepts and techniques. For instance, as students discover, the land-use problem in *Meadows or Malls?* involves solving systems of equations, understanding the geometry of how two-dimensional planes intersect in three-dimensional space, and developing and working with abstract notions such as identity element and inverse.

WHAT ABOUT DRILL AND PRACTICE?

Parents and teachers looking at a problem-based curriculum often wonder about skill development. Where, they ask, are the endless lists of problems that we all went through? How will students learn without such repetition?

Although IMP students first encounter an idea or algebraic technique through imaginative and challenging problems, they still need to practice it so that they don't have to rediscover it every time they need to use it. In this program, students are able to do this almost entirely in situations where they also need to think about mathematics. And because they construct ideas in context, instead of just memorizing definitions, mathematical concepts and methods have real meaning to them. They can, therefore, attain an appropriate level of fluency without the amount of practice needed by students for whom a technique is based just on memorization.

> In spite of studying these extra topics, IMP students are still having success with traditional tests.

For example, one of the fundamental ideas in algebra is the distributive property, which is used to simplify algebraic expressions. IMP students develop this principle in several ways, including area diagrams, numerical examples, and in the context of problem situations. After acquiring a basic idea of the principle, students have some routine practice with it, but they also use it repeatedly in the context of more complex situations. This approach makes the practice of procedures more interesting and more productive.

WHAT ABOUT RESULTS?

One test of success will be what happens to graduates of the Interactive Mathematics Program after they leave high school. A major long-term study currently under way—conducted by Norman Webb of the Wisconsin Center for Education Research—will provide important data on the program's effectiveness.

Some things we already know, however. For example, IMP students are staying with mathematics longer than students in traditional programs. Although nationally only 60 percent of all students take more than two years of high school mathematics (National Center for Education Statistics 1993), a significantly higher percentage of IMP students continue beyond two years (Webb et al. 1993). Considering that many students who would have otherwise gone into remedial mathematics classes are in the Interactive Mathematics Program, this finding takes on greater relevance. Other encouraging reports about the program indicate an increase in the number of minority and female students completing three years of college-qualifying mathematics.

One of the features of the program mentioned earlier is the expansion of the curriculum to include new topics. For example, students learn about normal distribution and standard deviation, regression and curve fitting, and matrix algebra for both equation solving and geometric transformations—areas of mathematics that most high school students never see. In spite of studying these extra topics, IMP students are still having success with traditional tests. Several studies have shown that they are doing at least as well as students in traditional mathematics classes on such tests as the SAT, even though IMP students spend far less time than do traditional students on algebra and geometry skills (IMP Evaluation Update 1995).

In another study of high schools with high concentrations of low-income and lower-achieving students, Interactive Mathematics students obtained greater achievement growth over the course of a school year than students in traditional general math and college preparatory courses (White et al. 1995). Student performance was measured by comparing pre- and post-test results on a mathematics achievement test composed of test items from the National Assessment of Educational Progress (NAEP).

We have been collecting anecdotal evidence on the program as well. Juan,[1] now age 19, graduated from an inner-city San Francisco high school and was the first person in his family to attend a university. He says the Interactive Mathematics Program helped prepare him for a college statistics class. "The topics in the textbook were all things I learned in IMP," he said.

After her first semester of a traditional college math course, Theresa, from San Antonio said,

> I always ask questions. The others don't. I thought it was because they knew it already, but then after class, they would ask me questions. I realized that they are just scared to ask. They don't know what is going on. Oh yes, I got an A.

Teachers also appreciate the curriculum. Over the years, we have worked with many talented teachers across the country who are now master IMP teacher/trainers in their own communities. Reflecting on their experience, a California teacher (Bussey 1992) wrote:

> Too many kids are flunking out of Algebra I or getting turned off to mathematics. Algebra I acts as a sieve, keeping only a select few, while filtering out many talented kids. Isn't there more than one way to "learn" mathematics and "do" mathematics? . . .
>
> When I'm in my classroom and witness my students working in groups, debating mathematical principles, and developing their own ideas to solve meaningful problems, that is when I feel most successful. My students have proven to me that they all can learn, that learning can be meaningful and relevant—and fun. What more can one ask of the educational process?

NOTE

1. Names are pseudonyms.

REFERENCES

Bussey, J. A. (1992). "Reflections of a Teacher Caught up in the Storm of Reform." Unpublished paper, West High School, Tracy, Calif.

IMP Evaluation Update. (Spring 1995). Emeryville, Calif.: The Interactive Mathematics Program, pp. 1–4.

National Center for Education Statistics. (May 1993). *Data Compendium for the NAEP 1992 Mathematics Assessment of the Nation and the States* (Report No. 23-ST04, pp. 398–399). Washington, D.C: U.S. Government Printing Office.

National Council of Teachers of Mathematics. (1989). *Curriculum and Evaluation Standards for School Mathematics.* Reston, Va.: NCTM.

Webb, N. L., H. Schoen, and S. D. Whitehurst. (April 1993). *Dissemination of Nine Precollege Mathematics Instructional Materials Projects Funded by the National Science Foundation 1981–91.* Madison: Wisconsin Center for Education Research, School of Education, University of Wisconsin-Madison.

White, P., A. Gamoran, and J. Smithson. (1995). *Math Innovations and Student Achievement in Seven High Schools in California and New York.* Madison: Consortium for Policy Research (CPRE) and Wisconsin Center for Education Research, School of Education, University of Wisconsin-Madison.

Resources

Center for Problem-Based Learning
Illinois Math and Science Academy
1500 W. Sullivan Road
Aurora, IL 60506
c/o Michelle Micetich
630-970-5956

Center for Problem-Based Learning
The College of William and Mary
Center for Gifted Education
Williamsburg, VA 23185
Joyce Van Tassel-Baska
757-221-2587

ASCD Service Center
Problem-Based Learning Network
800-933-2723

Authors

Lynne Alper is a professor of mathematics at San Francisco University. She can be reached at Interactive Mathematics Program, 6400 Hollis Street #5, Emeryville, California 94609.

Phyllis C. Blumenfeld is a professor in the School of Education, University of Michigan. She and her colleagues have written about projects in several journals including *Elementary School Journal, Journal of Learning Sciences,* and *Journal of Interactive Learning Environments.* Currently they are part of a national center funded by NSF, *Learning Technologies in Urban Schools,* that focuses on promoting inquiry through technology.

Ron Brandt is former executive editor at *Educational Leadership* and is now executive editor emeritus. He is also an education consultant.

Edwin M. Bridges is a professor of education for the School of Education, Stanford University. He has coauthored two books and numerous articles on problem-based learning. Professor Bridges is the 1996 recipient of the Roald F. Campbell Achievement Award in Educational Administration and a two time recipient of the Excellence in Teaching Award in the School of Education at Stanford.

Thomas M. Duffy is a professor of instructional systems technology and of language education at the School of Education, Indiana University. He is also the director of the undergraduate Corporate and Community Education Program.

Dan Fendel is a professor of mathematics at San Francisco University. He can be reached at Interactive Mathematics Program, 6400 Hollis Street #5, Emeryville, California 94609.

Sherry Fraser is a professor of mathematics at San Francisco University. She can be reached at Interactive Mathematics Program, 6400 Hollis Street #5, Emeryville, California 94609.

Shelagh Gallagher is professor for the gifted at the University of North Carolina at Charlotte and is director of a federally funded project, Problem-Based Learning in the Social Sciences.

Mark Guzdial is an assistant professor at Georgia Institute of Technology in the College of Computing and is part of the GVU Center and the EduTech Institute. His Web page is at http://www.cc.gatech.edu/gvu/people/faculty/Mark.Guzdial.html

Philip Hallinger is a professor of education and the director of the Vanderbilt Institute for Principals. He is also international research associate at Melborne University (Australia) and at Chiang Mai University (Thailand).

Andrew S. Hughes is a professor at the University of New Brunswick in Fredericton, Canada.

Joseph Krajcik, an associate professor of science education for the School of Education at the University of Michigan. He is an active member of the National Association of Research in Science Teaching and reviews manuscripts for a number of journals. He is to be the next President of the National Association for Research on Science Teaching (NARST).

Ronald Marx has been at the University of Michigan since fall of 1990. In that time, he has joined with an interdisciplinary group of colleagues (most notably, Phyllis Blumenfeld, Joe Krajcik, and Elliot Soloway) to conduct research and development on the pervasive uses of new technology in science education. They created the Center for Highly Interactive Computing in Education as an intellectual home and community for this work.

Fred M. Newmann is a professor of curriculum and instruction at the University of Wisconsin–Madison. He has extended this research on Authentic Instruction and reported results in a more recent publication: Authentic Achievement: Restructuring Schools for Intellectual Quality, San Francisco: Jossey-Bass, 1996.

Annemarie Palincsar completed her doctorate at the University of Illinois/Champaign-Urbana. She is on the faculty at the University of Michigan where she prepares teachers to work with heterogeneous classrooms of learners.

Erica Pearson has taught in Australia and England as well as the United States. She is presently teaching emotionally handicapped students in Richmond, Indiana.

Diane Resek is a professor of mathematics at San Francisco University. She can be reached at Interactive Mathematics Program, 6400 Hollis Street #5, Emeryville, California 94609.

John R. Savery, Ph.D., completed his doctorate at Indiana University, in Instructional Systems Technology and is currently teaching at DePaul University. He is the lead instructional application designer with the Academic Technology Development group and works with faculty to integrate instructional technology with effective pedagogy.

Joan M. Savoie teaches social studies at Fredericton High School in New Brunswick, Canada.

Elliot Soloway is a professor in the Department of Electrical Engineering and Computer Science and a professor in the School of Education at the University of Michigan. Previously, he was an associate professor in the Computer Science Department at Yale University.

William Stepien is the director of Consortium for Problem-Based Learning in Charlotte, North Carolina and the president of the firm Human Learning Resources in Charlotte, North Carolina.

Gary Wehlage is a professor of curriculum and instruction at the University of Wisconsin–Madison. He served as the associate director for the Center on Effective Secondary Schools and the Center on Organization and Restructuring of Schools.

David Workman is a Presidential Award winning science teacher at the Illinois Mathematics and Science Academy in Aurora, Illinois. He writes curriculum for integrated science and problem-based learning courses and has done research in gender issues in science education, problem-based learning, and integrated science.

Acknowledgments

Grateful acknowledgment is made to the following authors and agents for their permission to reprint copyrighted materials.

SECTION 1

Teachers College, Columbia University for "Problem-Based Learning in Medical and Managerial Education," by E. M. Bridges and P. Hallinger. In *Cognitive Perspectives on Educational Leadership*, by P. Hallinger, K. Leithwood, J. Murphy, (Eds.), pp. 253–267, 1993. Copyright © 1993 by Teachers College, Columbia University. Reprinted with permission. All rights reserved.

SECTION 2

Association for Supervision and Curriculum Development for "On Teaching for Understanding: A Conversation With Howard Gardner," by R. Brandt. From *Educational Leadership*, Vol. 50, No. 7, pp. 4–7, April 1993. Copyright © 1993 by ASCD. Reprinted with permission. All rights reserved.

Association for Supervision and Curriculum Development for "Five Standards of Authentic Instruction," by F. M. Newmann and G. G. Wehlage. From *Educational Leadership*, Vol. 50, No. 7, pp. 8–12, April 1993. Copyright © 1993 by ASCD. Reprinted with permission. All rights reserved.

Association for Supervision and Curriculum Development for "Problem-Based Learning: As Authentic as It Gets," by W. Stepien and S. Gallagher. From *Educational Leadership,* Vol. 50, No. 7, pp. 25–28, April 1993. Copyright © 1993 by ASCD. Reprinted with permission. All rights reserved.

Prufrock Press for "Content Acquisition in Problem-Based Learning: Depth Versus Breadth in American Studies," by S. A. Gallagher and W. J. Stepien. From *Journal for the Education of the Gifted,* Vol. 19, No. 3, pp. 257–275, 1996. Copyright © 1996 by Prufrock Press. Reprinted with permission. All rights reserved.

Educational Technology Publications, Inc. for "Problem Based Learning: An Instructional Model and Its Constructivist Framework," by J. R. Savery and T. M. Duffy. From *Educational Technology,* pp. 31–37, September-October 1995. Copyright © 1995 by Educational Technology Publications, Inc. Reprinted with permission. All rights reserved.

SECTION 3

Association for Supervision and Curriculum Development for "Problem-Based Learning as Classroom Solution," by J. M. Savoie and A. S. Hughs. From *Educational Leadership,* Vol. 52, No. 3, pp. 54–57, November 1994. Copyright © 1994 by ASCD. Reprinted with permission. All rights reserved.

Lawrence Erlbaum Associates, Inc. for "Motivating Project-Based Learning: Sustaining the Doing, Supporting the Learning," by P. C. Blumenfeld, E. Soloway, R. W. Marx, J. S. Krajcik, M. Guzdial, A. Palincsar. From *Educational Psychologist,* Vol. 26, No. 3 & 4, pp. 369–398, 1991. Copyright © 1991 by Lawrence Erlbaum Associates, Inc. Reprinted with permission. All rights reserved.

SECTION 4

Index

Stepien, William J., 22, 43–49,
    51–68, 141, 143–62, 185
Students
    demonstration of learning by,
        100
    empowering, as learners, 99
    preparation of, 12–13
    roles, 44–45
    social support for achieve-
        ments of, 38–39
    and technology, 121–27
    understanding of what
        they've learned, 25–36
Subject matter, organizing
    around problem, 97–99
Substantive conversation, 22,
    37–38

Task focus, 116

Teachers
    roles, 45, 116–20
    and technology, 127–30
Technical Education Research
    Center, 107
Technology, 120–30
Thorium problem, 43

Wehlage, Gary G., 22, 33–41,
    186
Wisconsin's Center on Organi-
    zation and Restructuring of
    Schools, 33
Workman, David, 141, 143–62,
    186

Young children, research on
    learning of very, 27–29

Notes

Notes

Notes

Notes

Notes

There are
one-story intellects,
   two-story intellects, and
     three-story intellects with skylights.

All fact collectors, who have no aim beyond their facts, are

      one-story minds.

     Two-story minds
   compare, reason, generalize,
   using the labors of the fact collectors
      as well as their own.

      Three-story minds
idealize, imagine, predict—their best illumination
comes from above,

       through the **skylight**.

—Oliver Wendell Holmes

SkyLight

PROFESSIONAL DEVELOPMENT

We Prepare Your Teachers Today
for the Classrooms of Tomorrow

Learn from Our Books and from Our Authors!

Ignite Learning in Your School or District.

SkyLight's team of classroom-experienced consultants can help you foster systemic change for increased student achievement.

Professional development is a process not an event. SkyLight's experienced practitioners drive the creation of our on-site professional development programs, graduate courses, research-based publications, interactive video courses, teacher-friendly training materials, and online resources—call SkyLight Professional Development today.

SkyLight specializes in three professional development areas.

Specialty # **Best Practices**

We **model** the best practices that result in improved student performance and guided applications.

Specialty # **Making the Innovations Last**

We help set up **support** systems that make innovations part of everyday practice in the long-term systemic improvement of your school or district.

Specialty # **How to Assess the Results**

We prepare your school leaders to encourage and **assess** teacher growth, **measure** student achievement, and **evaluate** program success.

Contact the SkyLight team and begin a process toward long-term results.

2626 S. Clearbrook Dr., Arlington Heights, IL 60005
800-348-4474 • 847-290-6600 • FAX 847-290-6609
info@skylightedu.com • www.skylightedu.com